Advances in Contemporary Educational Thought Series

Jonas F. Soltis, Editor

READING PRAGMATISM

CLEO H. CHERRYHOLMES

Teachers College, Columbia University
New York and London

Published by Teachers College Press, 1234 Amsterdam Avenue, New York, NY 10027

Library of Congress Cataloging-in-Publication Data

Cherryholmes, Cleo.
    Reading pragmatism / Cleo H. Cherryholmes.
       p.   cm. — (Advances in contemporary educational thought series ; v. 24)
    Includes bibliographical references (p.) and index.
    ISBN 0-8077-3847-6 (cloth). — ISBN 0-8077-3846-8 (paper)
    1. Education—Philosophy. 2. Postmodernism and education.
    3. Pragmatism. I. Title. II. Series.
    LB14.7.C44   1999
    370′.1—dc21   99-12634

ISBN 0-8077-3846-8 (paper)
ISBN 0-8077-3847-6 (cloth)

Printed on acid-free paper

Manufactured in the United States of America

06 05 04 03 02 01 00 99   8 7 6 5 4 3 2 1

To Mary, Diana, Tim, and Chris

Contents

Foreword

There is an intentional ambiguity in Cleo Cherryholmes' title for this book, *Reading Pragmatism*. It can mean reading *about* pragmatism: exploring various versions of this school of philosophy from Emerson, Peirce, and James to Dewey, Bernstein, and Rorty. This kind of "reading" would help one understand what pragmatism is by listening to many of the teachers in the pragmatist school. When reading the book this way, one sees Cherryholmes as one more teacher in the school presenting his own version, his own "reading" of what pragmatism is and can do. (Notice the shift here, from *reading about* pragmatism to presenting one's *reading of* pragmatism.) Reading the book this second way is to be treated to a sophisticated interpretation of a useful way to understand pragmatism in the context of contemporary educational theory, research, reform, and practice. The reader of this book will be enriched by both readings.

As he did in *Power and Criticism*, Cherryholmes makes the difficult readable and the opaque understandable. Whether explaining the analytic genealogy of Foucault, the deconstructions of Derrida, or the neopragmatism of Rorty, in good Peircean fashion, he "makes [their] ideas clear." Cherryholmes also brings helpful perspectives to our turbulent contemporary postmodern, poststructuralist, and postanalytic ways of thinking.

Throughout it all, Cherryholmes insists in his reading of pragmatism that we focus on the consequences of our conceptual frameworks, on the way they satisfy (or not) our purposes, our desires, our needs, and our attempts to make education better. Joining a few other contemporaries, Cherryholmes finds the aesthetic dimension to be the key ingredient in his reading of pragmatism. For Cherryholmes the pragmatist is first an artist using imagination and a sense of the beautiful, then an empiricist who looks to practical results—results that also must be beautiful and satisfying. Cherryholmes' pragmatist is also an inquirer and a doer embedded in a historical time, a particular culture, a changing society, and a community of inquiry. Power and democratic diversity, pluralism and fallibilism, become important ingredients in this exhilarating reading of pragmatism. Living and doing without certainty, without a firm foundation, without Truth, but with aesthetic and social imagination brings with it challenges and fulfillments rather than nihilism and despair.

This book explores, explains, and exposits an important stance toward contemporary educational thought that truly can help us advance in new ways to see old ideas and to find comfort in the uncomfortable intellectual climate of today and tomorrow.

Jonas F. Soltis
Series Editor

Acknowledgments

This book was written and re-written over several years. I had the opportunity to develop a number of these interpretations and arguments in several invited lectures in addition to imposing them on many unsuspecting yet gracious and helpful students in my classes. Chapter 2 was first given in lecture at the University of Northern Iowa at the invitation of John Smith and at the University of Granada, Spain at the invitation of Miguel Pereyra. Appendix B that operates as an outline for much of Part II was given in lecture at the Stockholm Institute of Education and the University of Orebro at the invitation of Tomas Englund. The major argument in Part III developed as a result of teaching policy analysis and was refined while lecturing and teaching at the University of Uppsala again at the invitation of Tomas Englund. The penultimate version of Part II was presented in colloquium at the University of Wisconsin at Madison at the invitation of Thomas Popkewitz. In addition to these public presentations that were so useful and instructive, I thank Thomas Popkewitz, Lynn Fendler, and other members of the Wednesday Group, Tomas Englund and his students and colleagues, and members of the late departed study group at Michigan State University.

This manuscript was largely completed following my transfer to the College of Education from the Department of Political Science at Michigan State University. I thank Carole Ames, Dean of Education, and Stephen Koziol, Chairperson of Teacher Education, for providing an atmosphere conducive to the exploration of ideas and writing. David Labaree, J. Bruce Burke, Robert Floden, Suzanne Wilson, and Richard Prawatt, in different ways, provided support, criticism, and opportunities for the exploration of many of these arguments.

Of course, major acknowledgments go to those whose work made this book possible, the American pragmatists; most importantly Charles Sanders Peirce, John Dewey, and W. V. O. Quine; as well as William James, Donald Davidson, and Richard Rorty, who has been very influential in drawing attention to pragmatism at the end of the century. In addition this reading of pragmatism would not have been possible without the work of the contemporary French theorists Michel Foucault and Jacques Derrida.

Finally, I thank my wife Mary, who has been consistently supportive and encouraging.

READING PRAGMATISM

Pragmatism after the better part of a century is once again attracting attention. Pragmatism looks simple at first glance. It is ferociously complex. This is one reading of pragmatism at the turn of the twenty-first century. Part I consists of two chapters. Chapter 1 outlines the task of reading pragmatism, very broadly. Chapter 2, for purposes of illustration, contrasts a pragmatist reading of *The Taxonomy of Educational Objectives* with three alternative readings as preface to a more detailed investigation.

CHAPTER 1

Introduction

WHY PRAGMATISM?

Why pragmatism? A short answer is that pragmatism looks to consequences that we endlessly bump up against. We respond to and live with outcomes all day, everyday. These results come from our actions and those of others. They also come from events beyond our control. Pragmatists anticipate outcomes. They look to imagined and actual outcomes. They look away from first principles such as those that might be advanced by any one of a variety of fundamentalisms. Pragmatists conceptualize the world where we, all of us, are constantly thrown forward as the present approaches but never quite reaches the future. Pragmatism is a discourse that attempts to bridge where we are with where we might end up. The future, the other unknown side of this bridge, can certainly be forbidding. There is little, if anything, that we can say with confidence about it. The temptation is to look to backward. Pragmatism resists this siren's song by accepting the challenge to look ahead.

WHY NOW?

Why pragmatism now? The date that pragmatist thought became recognizably coherent is debatable. Some writers, such as Cornel West (1989), trace it to Ralph Waldo Emerson (whom I do not discuss) in the first half of the nineteenth century and some, such as H. S. Thayer (1984), to Charles Sanders Peirce (whom I do discuss) in the last half of that century. Pragmatism was later articulated and developed, at the beginning of and in the early decades of the twentieth century, in the work of William James and John Dewey, each of whom I also draw upon.

But pragmatism was largely ignored by philosophers, educators, and social scientists during seven or so of the middle decades of the twentieth century, eclipsed by logical positivism and empiricism. In comparison with positivism and empiricism, pragmatism seemed soft-headed and ambiguous, insufficiently modern and scientific.[1] Today, positivism and empiricism are of little more than historical interest as intellectual schools of thought. This is not to say that their intellectual legacy is not to be found repeatedly in contemporary education. It is to say that almost no one—no one that I can identify—attempts to defend them rigorously and technically. At the end of their day, it was acknowledged that they posited untenable and unsupportable assumptions. They had asked logical argument, for example, to do things of which it was incapable (see Quine, 1953/1971, and Davidson, 1985, and the discussion of them in Chapter 13 below). Neither positivism nor empiricism is present in the story I tell. Their present-day use is, if I might say, pragmatic. It is appropriate to call pragmatism post-positivist and post-empiricist. It is also pre-positivist and pre-empiricist.

It is also arguable that pragmatism was ignored in mid-century because of the influence of structuralism, a school of thought that contributed much to twentieth-century studies in linguistics, anthropology, sociology, and literary theory, among other fields. It was a descriptive undertaking that attempted to identify the underlying organization of texts, practices, and the world. It also had prescriptive moments that attempted to prescribe and police social norms. Structuralism continues to exert a strong influence on educational thought and practice (see Cherryholmes, 1988, Chapter 2, for an argument to this point). But among the twentieth-century lessons that have been learned is that structuralist arguments continually undermine structuralist assumptions. Although structuralist templates for educational practice often seem intuitively quite attractive, they deconstruct (see Cherryholmes, 1988, Chapter 3). They deliver less than they promise. Poststructuralism and its associated genres of deconstruction, interpretive analytics, and new historicism take up, as it were, where structuralist endeavors break down. As they do so they generate powerful forms of interpretation and criticism. In practice one or several texts or practices are analyzed. These investigations, however, do not as a matter of course extend to the consequences of those texts and practices. Poststructural and postmodern investigations tend to be investigatory, interpretive, critical, and analytic. They are not forward-looking. They are oriented to commentary and criticism instead of consequences and action. Poststructuralism and its postmodernist relatives do not have a project that looks to action, nor do they seek one (see Lilla, 1998, for an extended discussion of this point).

Pragmatism looks to results. First principles, foundational assumptions, fundamentalist beliefs, and fully rationalized practices are not on its agenda. What is pragmatism? Imagine a conversation. Imagine a series of questions that an interlocutor (Q) might put to a pragmatist (P) followed by her answers.

Q: Pragmatism, I have heard, is about consequences and doing things. Let's begin with doing things. Why do we do what we do?

P: To get results.

Q: What kind of results?

P: Those that are satisfying and fulfilling.

Q: Where do we get our conceptions of satisfaction and fulfillment?

P: We construct them.

Q: How?

P: From experience. From experiences that are political, social, linguistic, cultural, racial, and gendered, for example.

Q: Are these conceptions of satisfaction and fulfillment stable?

P: No. They change. We compose conceptions of satisfaction and fulfillment. They are interpreted and criticized anew as we move from situation to situation. They are constantly being rewritten.

Q: If our goals are not stable, what about our projections and constructions of consequences and knowledge? How much confidence can we place in them?

P: They are fallible. As situations change, our store of knowledge and its application becomes problematic.

Q: How do you propose to cope with changing conceptions of satisfaction and desire and with knowledge and methodologies that fail?

P: Subject them to multiple interpretations, expose them to criticism and to the discipline and competition of different conceptions and beliefs.

Q: How do we choose? How do we choose among conflicting conceptions of satisfaction, desire, and beauty, and among beliefs, methodologies, and technologies?

P: Inclusively. In democratic solidarity and not by appealing to foundational and fundamentalist principles. We increase the risk of making unsatisfactory choices to the extent that "other" conceptions, beliefs, individuals, and groups are excluded and silenced.

Q: This sounds very idealistic. Is pragmatism simply a rhetoric of wishing our way through life? Is it just wishful thinking? What about power and oppression? Inequality and subjugation? Social dominance and submission?

P: At the beginning and end of the day pragmatists are realists because they value what happens. They are interested in results, in consequences. They understand that pragmatist experiments are social constructions. These constructions come from experience and ideas and knowledge and power. Proposed material/ideal and realistic/idealistic distinctions deconstruct because the material conditions in which we find ourselves contribute to and shape what we can conceptualize and enact. Pragmatists try to bring about beautiful results in the midst of power and oppression and ignorance.

Think of pragmatists as artists, if you will. They are artists who seek to generate beauty and satisfaction in the context and circulation of power.

Their productions are never finished. They are interpreted, reinterpreted, and criticized indefinitely. As a result, they are continually open to new experiences and problems and opportunities. Pragmatist productions deconstruct, they do indeed. And their deconstruction invites, indeed requires, revision and replacement. This reading is an exploration in thinking about consequences.[2]

READING PRAGMATISM

What does it mean to *read?* The *Oxford English Dictionary (OED)* lists the following definitions of the verb *read*: "To consider, interpret, discern, etc."; "To have an idea; to think or suppose that, etc."; "To make out or discover the meaning or significance of; to declare or expound this to another." The *OED* assigns the following definition to the noun *reading*: "The act of interpreting or expounding." Readers produce readings. Different readers produce different readings. One thing this reading is not—it is not offered as dogma or ideology, even though my prose may at times give that impression.

Two pragmatist texts are highlighted at the outset. The first is Peirce's pragmatic maxim. Here is the 1905 version:

> The method prescribed in the [pragmatic] maxim is to trace out in the imagination the conceivable practical consequences—the consequences for deliberate, self-controlled conduct—of the affirmation or denial of the concept; and the assertion of the maxim is that herein lies the *whole* of the purport of the word, the *entire* concept. (Peirce, 1905/1984, p. 494, emphasis in original)

The second is Dewey's first chapter from *Art as Experience* from 1934. This reading sets them in the context of contemporary social theory and criticism. I return to them repeatedly. Because readings are interpretations, they are context- and purpose-dependent. And readers as interpreters stand in relation to their time and place. Readers of pragmatism and anything else in different times and places produce different interpretations. This is one effect of *differance*, as a student of Derrida might remind us.

This reading, obviously, is from my time and place. It is a pragmatist reading pragmatism. I agree with Thomas McLaughlin (1990) that "interpretation—the process of producing textual meaning—is . . . rhetorical. It does not live in a realm of certain truths; it lives in a world where only constructions of the truth are possible, where competing interpretations argue for supremacy" (p. 7). Pragmatism rejects the possibility of essentialist readings that try to identify what a text "really" means (see Chapter

5). This reading, then, is a rhetorical and pragmatic exercise in enacting that for which it argues. It is an exploration in thinking about consequences. It is also someone reading for the consequences of pragmatism.[3]

WHY THIS READING?

Previously I have argued for a critical pragmatism (see Cherryholmes, 1988, Chapter 8). In that discussion I used the word *critical* to qualify pragmatism because the word *pragmatism* had arguably become debased. The word *pragmatism* had seemingly been subverted by constant and popular usages that were far removed from its classical versions in the work of, say, Peirce. Pragmatism seemed to mean a thorough lack of principle, exaggerated expediency, emphasis on monetary gain, crassness and vulgarity in the "calculation" of consequences, and to be something bounded by a horizon of immediacy. I used the phrase *vulgar pragmatism* to refer to those interpretations. For my purposes I turned to a critical pragmatism. I sought to prevent individuals from using pragmatism as a cover for work that was crass, expedient, and short-sighted. Times change. It does not now seem that the vulgar and mechanical technicians among us will gain much by cloaking themselves with claims of pragmatism. Having distinguished between critical and vulgar pragmatism and acknowledging that this distinction deconstructs (see Henderson, 1989, and Cherryholmes, 1989, for an exchange on this point), I retain criticism here as only one of many constituents of pragmatism. In the reading of pragmatism that follows, I fold the ideas that constituted what I called critical pragmatism into a larger view that focuses more heavily on aesthetics and power.

The earlier distinction between critical and vulgar pragmatism deconstructs because each requires the other for its existence and coherence. Likewise, distinctions between the categories aesthetic/nonaesthetic and art/nonart that I use here deconstruct as well. I foreground aesthetics and art, but in doing so I do not propose new structural distinctions. I argue for a broadly aesthetic way of thinking about and living in the world. In the history of pragmatist thought it is arguable that when James advocated the "cash value" of an idea, he perhaps unintentionally advocated a conception of pragmatism that invited a truncated and misleading reading, a reading that emphasized short-term gain. I, along with McDermott (1981), Shusterman (1992, 1997), Garrison (1995, 1997), Jackson (1995), and Fesmire (1995), emphasize aesthetics. In addition, this reading of pragmatism sets the art and aesthetics of ordinary experience in the midst of power.[4] Power is used to refer to asymmetric relationships among individuals and groups where some benefit and are rewarded and others are penalized and deprived. Power circulates in micro and macro transactions, in both face to face interactions as in a classroom and in institutional processes as in state legislative deliberations. It is in the context of social transactions and minor and major social inequalities that our aesthetic conceptions are formed and our convictions in what it is most reasonable to believe are established. Power, aesthetics, and knowledge, not necessarily is this or any stable order or set of interactions, produce anticipations of consequences that we continually re-write and re-evaluate.

AN OUTLINE OF THE READING AND THE BOOK

I begin by demonstrating a pragmatist reading. In the next chapter, four alternative readings of the influential Bloom, Engelhart, Furst, Hill, and Krathwohl (1956) *Taxonomy of Educational Objectives* are presented, a book chosen because of its enormous influence on educational practice over the last half century or so. It is well and widely known. This allows me to demonstrate one pragmatist approach to reading before I turn to reading pragmatism itself. Four readings of the Taxonomy are presented, beginning with an attempt to draw out the intention of its authors. Then I move to readings that employ Foucault's interpretive analytics and Derrida's deconstruction. Finally, the Taxonomy is read as a pragmatist exercise. The consequences of reading it as a pragmatist experiment are quite at odds with approaching it as a defining structuralist monument.

The three chapters in Part II present my overview of pragmatism. The operative assumption for this reading comes from Peirce's maxim—the meaning of a concept is found by "trace[ing] out in the imagination the conceivable practical consequences . . . of the affirmation or denial of the concept" (1905/1984, p. 494). James and Dewey extended the pragmatic view of meaning to actions. The chapter then builds on Dewey's argument in *Art as Experience*. Pragmatists are active in anticipating and shaping outcomes. They wish to bring about results that are desirable and satisfying. Pragmatists inexorably are pulled toward thinking about the world in terms of art and aesthetics because exercising our imagination is itself artistic. Chapter 4 places these artistic and aesthetic endeavors in the social context of their construction. Pragmatists are artists whose constraints and opportunities present themselves in social structures and in the exercise and effects of power. If we are rational and reasonable in the way that we and others contemplate the future, then, the argument goes, we will support democratic institutions and processes because we wish to expand our conceptions of consequences. Democratic inclusiveness and freedom of expression both shape the formulation of aesthetic images and operate to expose ugly and unwanted courses of action. Chapter 5 turns away from aesthetics and its social construction to philosophical assumptions or their denial, that characterizes pragmatism. Pragmatism is inductive. It anticipates where we might go from where we are. The properties of inductive argument lead pragmatists to reject essentialism, representationalism, and foundationalism. These characteristics of pragmatism, as I read them, describe a poststructural way of looking at the world.

Part III shifts from reading pragmatism to reading research pragmatically. If it is the case that the meaning of a conception is found in its conceivable practical consequences, then it follows that the meaning of research findings that we constantly consume and produce is found in their conceivable consequences. This may be easy to say, but it is harder to do. What does it mean to read research findings for their conceivable consequences? These chapters detail a pragmatist investigation into the meaning of reciprocal teaching, that Palincsar and Brown (1984) described in a widely celebrated article. It is obvious that conceivable consequences are made possible and limited by what one can conceive. What one can conceive depends, in turn, upon one's experiences, values, interests, knowledge, and aesthetic sensibilities.

Chapter 6 outlines issues involved in pragmatist readings, such as rejecting the possibility of a fundamentalist or foundational reading. It also provides a brief summary of the reciprocal teaching study. But recapitulating research findings does not fix their meaning. Chapters 7, 8, and 9 demonstrate some of what is involved in tracing conceivable practical consequences of reciprocal teaching. Three readings of this research are provided from the perspectives of an ecological feminist, critical educator, and deconstructionist. It is not surprising that they do not converge. It is a bit surprising that the first two contradict each other. Chapter 10 readdresses issues raised in chapter 3. This time as reflections on these three pragmatist readings. Given that various people value consequences of the same idea or action differently, what are we to do? My pragmatist response is that we, in democratic solidarity, are best off behaving as artists. We should develop, criticize, negotiate, and promote our visions of what is fulfilling and satisfying. We should construct beautiful outcomes as we see them. I show that (1) meanings of ideas and actions and (2) statements that operate as true ceaselessly merge and diverge. The fluidity of meaning and truth, in addition to the effects of power, is an important constituent of the aesthetic assessment of consequences.

Part IV sets pragmatism in the context of modernity and postmodernity. It links pragmatism to analytic philosophy and shows how program evaluations have had the cumulative effect of returning, if often unnoticed, to pragmatist assumptions and orientations. Chapter 11 outlines character-istics of modernity and its relation to postmodernity. Modern and post-modern themes broadly characterize the times in which we live. They have been at work creating the present for the past few hundred years. It is within this historical setting that the appeal and persuasiveness of pragmatism becomes so palpable and understandable. Chapter 12 sets pragmatism in the context of analytic philosophy. An autobiographical note is appropriate at this point. It was reading W. V. O. Quine's (1953/ 1971) "Two Dogmas of Empiricism," that I discuss in chapter 12, that brought me into the pragmatist camp. His argument and that of his student, Donald Davidson (1985), in "On the Very Idea of a Conceptual Scheme," are key to my understanding and reading of pragmatism. These are the doors through which I passed in arriving at John Dewey's (1934/ 1980) *Art as Experience* (the reverse chronology may be of interest to some). Chapter 13 reviews Michael Fullan's (1991) *The New Meaning of Educational Change,* that is a review of hundreds of program evaluations of educational change efforts. He concludes his review of empirical (not to be confused with empiricist) findings by describing pragmatist tenets as the road to successful change. I set the analytic arguments in Chapter 12 beside the empirical findings of Chapter 13 to dramatize the fact that developments in logic and empirical research simultaneously converged on, or some might say slouched toward, pragmatism.

Part V consists of chapter 14. It is a reprise and extension of the reading.

CHAPTER 2

Pragmatism and a Problem of Reading: Revisiting The Taxonomy of Educational Objectives

To some degree readings are always contested because they are generated relative to the perspectives of different readers. Thus, one should not expect as a matter of course that alternative readings will agree. Even though pragmatism cannot be personalized in the form of an individual reader, it too has a perspective, a family of perspectives as it were. Four readings of the Taxonomy are offered as prelude to a more extended reading of pragmatism. One pragmatist reading is contrasted to one that seeks to identify authorial intention, to one suggested by Michel Foucault that reads for a genealogy of the text, and to one influenced by Jacques Derrida that reads for meanings and textual movements that presage deconstruction.

THE TAXONOMY

In 1948 the American Psychological Association began a project to classify educational objectives. The effort was headed by Benjamin Bloom and culminated with the publication of *The Taxonomy of Educational Objectives*. Bloom's influence was so great that the Taxonomy is often referred to as "Bloom's Taxonomy." The authors stated that their "major purpose in constructing a Taxonomy of educational objectives is to facilitate communication" (p. 10) among those "who deal with curricular and evaluation problems" (p. 1). They added:

> The major task in setting up any kind of Taxonomy is that of selecting appropriate symbols, giving them precise and usable definitions, and securing the consensus of the group which is to use them. Similarly, developing a classification of educational objectives requires the selection of an appropriate

list of symbols to represent all the major types of educational outcomes. (p. 11)

They set out to classify "student behaviors that represented the intended outcomes of the educational process" (p. 12) that are distinct from teacher behaviors and actual student behaviors.

Minimally a Taxonomy is a classificatory scheme "designating classes of objects where the members of a class have something in common" (p. 10). But a Taxonomy is more than simple classification:

> A Taxonomy must be so constructed that the order of the terms must corre-
> spond to some "real" order among the phenomena represented by the terms
> . . . [and be] validated by demonstrating its consistency with the theoretical
> views in research findings of the field it attempts to order. (p. 17)

Even though it was not possible to base the Taxonomy on existing theories of personality and learning, the authors hoped that it would point toward general theories that would follow. It has had a remarkably wide-ranging impact on education internationally as well as in the United States during the decades since its publication. It has influenced curriculum design and development, textbook organization and writing, conditioned approaches to sales, and preservice and inservice teacher education programs; provided outlines for dominant approaches to lesson and unit designs; and guided the construction and evaluation of many standardized assessment tests. It was a remarkable achievement. Because of the Taxonomy's professional and historical importance it, again, invites attention.

THE TAXONOMY AS A STATEMENT
OF AUTHORIAL INTENTION

The intention of the American Psychological Association seems clear enough. They wanted to modernize thinking about education by rationalizing what schools taught, an ongoing concern. One operative assumption was that scientific and legitimate knowledge is structural and hierarchical. A second assumption was that structured and organized knowledge is what schools should be teaching. A third assumption was that everyone—including educators, students, evaluators, and society at large—would be better off if it were possible to think about such knowledge in a structured way. A few of their guiding principles are insightful about subsequent uses to which the Taxonomy would be put.

1. "The Taxonomy ... should reflect, in large part, the distinctions teachers make between student behaviors" (p. 13).
2. "The Taxonomy should be logically developed and internally consistent" (p. 14).
3. "The Taxonomy should be consistent with our present understanding of psychological phenomena" (p. 14).
4. "The classification should be a purely descriptive scheme in which every type of educational goal can be represented in a relatively neutral fashion ... by avoiding terms which implicitly convey value judgments and by making the Taxonomy as inclusive as possible" (p. 14).
5. "A comprehensive Taxonomy of educational objectives must, in our opinion, include all the educational objectives represented in American education without making judgments about their value, meaningfulness, or appropriateness." (p. 30)

The taxonomy of cognitive objectives has six levels.

Levels of Cognitive Objectives

1.00 Knowledge
2.00 Comprehension
3.00 Application
4.00 Analysis
5.00 Synthesis
6.00 Evaluation

Higher levels of the hierarchy cognitively subsumed lower levels: "The objectives in one class are likely to make use of and be built on the behaviors found in the preceding classes in this list" (p. 18). They were arranged from simple to complex, concrete to abstract. The ideas that the authors of the Taxonomy promoted may or may not have been new or widely shared in the 1950s, but they seemingly are believed in one form or another by many educators today. There are other ways, however, of reading the Taxonomy.

THE TAXONOMY AS AN OBJECT OF HISTORY

We live in modern times. The term *modernity* is often used to refer to the rationalization of Western societies that began with the Enlightenment and the rise of modern science in the seventeenth and eighteenth centuries (see Chapter 12 for a longer discussion of modernity). Distinctions between what is modern and nonmodern are often summed up by a series of binary distinctions with the valued term preceding the disvalued term. Here is one such list:

Modern/Nonmodern

Objective/Subjective
Fact/Value
Knowledge/Politics (Ideology)
Science/Religion
Theory/Practice
Rational Freedom/Causal Necessity
Performances/Happenings
Active/Passive
Creative/Repetitive

Modern ways of looking at the world value attempts to be objective in the search for knowledge and control. In this sense the Taxonomy is a thoroughly modern document and is an object of history. It is an object of historical developments that began several hundred years ago.

Michel Foucault gave a particularly interesting reading of modernity that I extend to the Taxonomy. A French intellectual who called himself a historian of systems of ideas, Foucault studied historical practices that made the production of specialized discursive practices possible. These practices included those that constitute modern prisons, mental institutions, hospitals, sexuality, and political economy and general grammar. He argued that social and political institutions and discursive practices are mutually productive and reproductive. He wrote:

> Discursive practices are not purely and simply ways of producing discourse. They are embodied in technical processes, in institutions, in patterns for general behavior, in forms for transmission and diffusion, and in pedagogical forms which, at once, impose and maintain them. (Foucault, 1980a, p. 200)

Foucault was interested in the political production of truth. How are modern discourses constituted? How do discourses constitute institutions? How do institutions, in turn, constitute and regulate discourses? He tried to account for how texts came to be what they are and not to "explain" or "interpret" them or to say what they "really" meant. He described long, slow, almost imperceptible changes in discursive practices, occasionally interspersed with jarring disjunctures, that constituted meaning in sign systems. It is inescapable, he argued, that discourses are materially produced by specific social, political, and economic arrangements. What is said in the name of truth is not simply an idealist construction. Discursive practices have a material basis because they cannot be extricated from their historical setting. A discursive practice is

> a body of anonymous, historical rules, always determined in the time and space that have defined a given period, and for a given social, economic, geographical, or linguistic area, the conditions of operation of the enunciative function. (Foucault, 1972, p. 117)

The rules of a discourse govern what is said and what remains unsaid. They identify who can speak with authority and who must listen. They are anonymous because there is no identifiable author (Foucault, 1980a) and they do not have a clear-cut beginning (Said, 1975).

Implications of this argument for contemporary education are striking and dramatic. Many professional educators, such as the authors of the Taxonomy, might choose to believe that they are in control of what they say and do and that their discourses-practices are based on true statements. But if truth is discursive and discourses are historically situated, then truth cannot be spoken in the absence of power. Each historical arrangement of power has its own truths. Foucault summarizes the relationship between truth and power in the following passage:

> Truth is a thing of this world: it is produced only by virtue of multiple forms of constraint. And it induces regular effects of power. Each society has its regime of truth, its "general politics" of truth: that is, the types of discourse which it accepts and makes function as true; the mechanisms and instances which enable one to distinguish true and false statements, the means by which each is sanctioned; the techniques and procedures accorded value in the acquisition of truth; the status of those who are charged with saying what counts as true. (1980b, p. 131)

Discourses dominant in a historical period and geographical location determine what counts as true, important, relevant; what gets spoken; and what remains unsaid. Discourses are generated and governed by rules and power. It is not possible to separate the meaning of signs, such as the Taxonomy, and sign systems from their production and reproduction. It may be that the relationship of a word to a definition or concept is arbitrary—for example, many words could be used to signify the same objects or ideas—but such arbitrary configurations are the products of and are fixed by history, culture, politics, economics, and language. Individuals are linked to macro-social processes and institutions when they become socialized, and by this mechanism power helps shape how we think of ourselves and act. Power shapes subjective feelings and beliefs—our subjectivities. Often power is most effective and efficient when it operates as desire because desire often makes effects of power invisible.

I think of power in terms of asymmetrical relationships by which some people are rewarded and indulged and others are deprived and sanctioned (see Cherryholmes, 1988, Chapter 1). Power circulates in the transactions that constitute these relationships, and social institutions are shaped when these relationships become sedimented and routinized—they often look as natural as trees and rocks. In Foucault's analysis, discursive and nondiscursive practices of, say, schools, teacher education programs, school board elections, state certification requirements, and textbook adoption procedures create and re-create asymmetries as individuals desire to become the best they can be as teachers, administrators, counselors, or supervisors. Power shapes and informs our psyche. We are objects of social institutions and processes as we intentionally engage in meaningful behavior. Foucault argued that the political production of truth is generated by individuals as they become caught up and proficient in discursive and nondiscursive practices of their time. They participate in discourses and social practices without origins or authors and over which they have little control. Given his analysis, a progressive politics for Foucault (1973) is: How can people gain control of their discourses and practices instead of being controlled by them?

Turning to the Taxonomy, a Foucauldian analyst might argue that it is difficult to imagine how the Taxonomy could have turned out differently in the United States in the 1950s. The effects of power, the argument goes, speak Truth through the Taxonomy. Modern professions, for example, normalize and police their discourses and practices. To advance themselves, professions—in this case, professional education—attempt to extend the scope of their rationalizing activities as they enlarge their body of proprietary knowledge, expertise, and practice. In this sense the construction of a taxonomy of educational objectives by a committee of the American Psychological Association was a quintessential modern activity. It continued conversations and discourses that had existed for some 300 years or so. After accepting the task of constructing a taxonomy, the shape of the final text was largely a foregone conclusion. It would be logically ordered and hierarchical, and it would allow educators to classify their thinking and work into clear-cut categories. In short, it would order their professional world for them. From a Foucauldian perspective it is fitting to view the intentions of the authors of the Taxonomy and their subjectivities as objects of history, as objects constituted by the modern times in which we live. Thus the Taxonomy represents an historically and culturally provincial way of looking at knowledge, education, and society.

Disregarding whether the Taxonomy truly expressed the subjective intentions of its authors or was simply another historical event in the long, drawn-out modernization of the West, it is fair to ask whether the authors of the Taxonomy were successful in their attempt to rationalize educational objectives. Were they successful on their own terms?

THE TAXONOMY AS A DECONSTRUCTING TEXT

Deconstruction is associated with the work of Jacques Derrida. He has argued and continues to argue that meaning is not centered or fixed because it is caught in a play of words and definitions. In this view texts, including the Taxonomy and its proposed structure, only give the appearance of stability. Two provocative deconstructive arguments are to the effect that meanings (1) are dispersed throughout language and texts and (2) are deferred in time. If meanings are dispersed and deferred, then the assertion that meanings are fixed is an illusion; this would also apply to the meanings of words and concepts that constitute the Taxonomy. Textual claims and meanings turn against themselves by subverting their rhetorical and structural claims. An example of how meanings are dispersed is found in the way that we use dictionaries to find the meaning of a word. A definition of a word turns into a series of words, each with its own definition, these definitions point to yet further definitions, and so on indefinitely. Deferral of meaning is closely related to dispersal of meaning. If the search for meanings can be pursued indefinitely throughout the language, then it is constantly extended and deferred into the future.

Does the Taxonomy deconstruct? I begin by noting the authors' concession that knowledge and information are relative. They write:

> It should also be noted that the validity, accuracy, and meaningfulness of information are relative in many ways and always are related to a particular period of time. . . . There is also a geographical and cultural aspect to knowledge in the sense that what is known to one group is not necessarily known to another group, class, or culture. . . . Truth and knowledge are only relative and . . . there are no hard and fast truths which exist for all time and all places. (p. 32)

> All knowledge is partial. (p. 40)

The effect of these comments—and they demonstrate a sophisticated and subtle grasp of important issues—undermines the Taxonomy. Briefly, it goes like this:

1. All knowledge and information is relative to time and place and is partial.
2. The Taxonomy provides knowledge and information to educators.
3. Therefore the Taxonomy is relative to time and place and is partial.

At several places the relationship between the Taxonomy and its place in history and geography are mentioned. This generates an important contradiction. The Taxonomy is used to support existing educational units and programs

> We are of the opinion that the major distinctions between classes should reflect, in large part, the distinctions teachers make among student behaviors. (p. 13)

> A final criterion is that the Taxonomy must be accepted and used by the workers in the field if it is to be regarded as a useful and effective tool. (p. 24)

These statements support existing educational structures and processes, while elsewhere the authors claim to be value-neutral:

> A comprehensive Taxonomy of educational objectives must, in our opinion, include all the educational objectives represented in American education without making judgments about their value, meaningfulness, or appropriateness. (p. 30)

The Taxonomy was designed to be used in contemporary educational practice, and that practice was never criticized. The activities, rules, values, ideologies, and power arrangements of contemporary educational practice were not made explicit or questioned. The Taxonomy, then, was relative to what would facilitate school operation in the United States of the 1950s. The Taxonomy declared itself to be value-neutral while simultaneously admitting that it is relative to historical practices, ideologies, and power arrangements. It was designed to serve interests of the status quo while claiming to be neutral in the name of educational expertise.

The Taxonomy also deconstructs in its claims about values. The authors write about level 6.00: "It is quite possible that the evaluative process will in some cases be the prelude to the acquisition of new knowledge, a new attempt at comprehension or application, or a new analysis or synthesis" (p. 185). They concede, therefore, that evaluation precedes knowledge and comprehension and other levels lower in the Taxonomy. If evaluation precedes the knowledge level of the Taxonomy, then the application of the Taxonomy cannot be value-free, again undercutting its claim of value-neutrality.

Higher levels of the Taxonomy were supposed to subsume lower levels. This would make it possible to arrange learning objectives and experiences from simple to complex and concrete to abstract: "As we have defined them, the objectives in one class are likely to make use of and be built on the behaviors found in the preceding classes in this list" (p. 18). The Taxonomy was built on binary distinctions such as: comprehension/knowledge, application/comprehension, analysis/application, synthesis/analysis, and evaluation/synthesis, where the first term in each pair is valued over the second because the second is subsumed and thereby superseded by the first. But sometimes the order is reversed. We have just reviewed the authors' admission that knowledge objectives do not always precede evaluation objectives. Comprehension can also precede knowledge because if one cannot comprehend, translate, and interpret certain messages, some kinds of knowledge cannot be learned. Likewise, application sometimes precedes comprehension because only after successful application is comprehension demonstrated and to assert that one of this pair always precedes the other is to be dogmatic in the extreme.

Level 4.00—analysis—"emphasizes the breakdown of the material into its constituent parts and detection of the relationships of the parts and of the way they are organized" (p. 144). This definition, it turns out, is a description of a diagram of problem solving (p. 121) offered as an example of application. Sometimes one can only apply knowledge and information after analysis by breaking knowledge and information into constituent parts. Synthesis "is here defined as the putting together of elements and parts so as to form a whole" (p. 162). This is the other side of analysis. Are we interested in defining the whole in terms of its parts or in looking at the parts that constitute the whole? Choosing whether analysis precedes or follows synthesis depends upon context, purpose, situation, background experiences, and so forth. Bloom and colleagues concede that evaluation sometimes precedes knowledge. This can be generalized to the rest of the Taxonomy. Movement from complex to simple and abstract to concrete occurs, as well as the other way around. Additionally, evaluation precedes knowledge because one only decides what to learn or know as a result of a decision, and decisions cannot be made without reference to value(s). Choices are relative to values.

The Taxonomy deconstructs in terms of many of its most important ambitions and claims. From this perspective it makes little difference whether the Taxonomy was an expression of its authors' intentions or another step in the continuing process of modernization because (1) if it is read as an expression of its authors' intentions, it failed, and (2) if it is read as a rationalization of education, it failed. It is possible, however, to read the Taxonomy in yet another way that capitalizes on these insights.

THE TAXONOMY AS A PRAGMATIST EXERCISE

Pragmatism offers a dramatic alternative to the foregoing readings. For purposes of demonstration I draw upon that part of Peirce's (1905/1984) pragmatic maxim where the meaning of a concept, the Taxonomy in this case, is found in "trace[ing] out in the imagination the conceivable practical consequences—the consequences for deliberate, self-controlled conduct—of the affirmation or denial of the concept" (p. 494). Disregarding whether one is concerned with the author's intentions, the genealogy of the Taxonomy, or the manner in which it deconstructs, the consequences of affirming and acting on it have thus far been ignored. Think of the Taxonomy as an experiment, as artistic artifact. Does it produce desirable outcomes? Is the Taxonomy as *objet d'art* satisfying?

Pragmatism is not programmatic. It does not promote a systematic logic or methodology. It offers guidelines rather than system and method. If one affirms the Taxonomy by acting on it, does it produce desirable consequences? What kind of educational practices are created? Are these practices appealing? Do they promote satisfaction? Do they point toward a good way of school and life? It is useful to think holistically and contextually in assessing the educational production of the Taxonomy so that the likelihood of overlooking nonobvious consequences will be lessened. Promoting democracy and tolerance also expands the number of conceivable outcomes by increasing the likelihood that those who are different from us will think of something that we have not. And avoiding essentialist and foundationalist assumptions opens up what can be thought because many areas of thought are closed off if one believes that one knows the Truth.

Instead of seeing the Taxonomy as a cognitive imperative that is designed to structure disciplinary knowledge or as the result of a historical era or as a self-undermining text, a pragmatist asks what the conceivable consequences of acting on it are. If one were to list an array of possible consequences of employing the Taxonomy, then pragmatism becomes little more than an academic exercise. The point for pragmatists is to assess the consequences in terms of making life better or worse, more pleasurable or more painful, more productive or more unproductive. I refer to these as aesthetic issues because they deal with satisfaction and fulfillment, that in turn determine whether our educational practices and schools are acceptable.

Here are some consequences of enacting the Taxonomy:

1. It promotes organizational inequality and hierarchy.
2. It allows knowledge, curriculum, instruction, and evaluation to be organized structurally.
3. It complements and reinforces modernizing trends in education that value specialization, fragmentation, individualization, accountability, and rationalization.
4. It gives the authority to make decisions about knowledge, curriculum, instruction, and evaluation to experts—academic experts, professional educators, and those who find themselves at the higher levels of professional organizations.
5. It legitimizes the policing and evaluating of instruction.
6. It reinforces and is reinforced by modernist tendencies among modern professions.
7. It provides a medium through which the power of the profession can shape individual professional subjectivities as teachers build their practice around the Taxonomy.
8. It fails to deliver on some of its promises because it is arbitrary and circular.

Here are some consequences of denying the authority of the Taxonomy:

1. One can pursue the Taxonomy's objectives in a circular and roundabout fashion, say from analysis to application and back to analysis, instead of moving from one educational objective to another, say from the concrete to the abstract, in a linear and hierarchical manner.
2. It is possible playfully to reorder and rearrange educational objectives because the purpose and context of instruction determine how to proceed and purposes and contexts are, seemingly, never stable.
3. The role of teachers as curriculum planners becomes elevated.
4. The experiences students bring with them contribute more explicitly to the context for instruction and the ordering of educational objectives.
5. Instruction can be designed to follow the Taxonomy's hierarchy and categories as originally listed or as they might be rearranged or dispensed with them altogether.
6. Educational practice will not be based on a self-deconstructing

structure that some would be inclined to read as foundational to teaching.

Pragmatically speaking, the Taxonomy is one of many texts that teachers can use. Order and organization certainly have a place in education, but the playfulness that comes from denying order also has educational value. Any claims that the Taxonomy lays bare the structure of cognitive knowledge or that it is the most appropriate structure for organizing classroom lessons are exaggerated. It is a tool to be used in the service of where we want to go. The Taxonomy, for a pragmatist, is valuable if it contributes to desired outcomes. It is not valuable if it becomes a straightjacket for planning and instruction. Does it help us get where we want to go? Where do we want to go?

CONCLUSION

What can be learned from these readings?

1. Intelligent, well-educated, conscientious, and industrious authors produce texts that are products of time and place. Their texts, at best, are but partial accounts of their subjects.
2. Texts that present themselves as natural, as textbooks often do, are deceptive and misleading.
3. Insofar as we believe that our texts are modern and rational and noncontradictory, we deceive ourselves as well as others because they deconstruct—sometimes in ways that are important to what we wish to do, sometimes in ways that are unimportant.
4. We should be cautious whenever we are tempted to claim that our texts are accurate, correct, truthful, logically consistent, and authoritative.
5. Our texts and taxonomies are more and less useful to the degree that they produce the consequences we desire by promoting the kind of society in which we wish to live and helping us live our lives as we wish (utility is relative to purpose).

Do not be misled. *This does not mean* that anything goes—not at all. *This does mean* that arguments such as those found in the Taxonomy deconstruct, are partial and incomplete, are ideologically committed, and are relative to time and place. If we are careful and honest about what we read and write, then subtexts and contexts will sometimes become main texts as we share with our readers and students the complexities of reading and writing about how we should live. These choices are made daily.

READING PRAGMATISM: AESTHETICS/KNOWLEDGE/POWER

Much of Part II is one reading of Peirce's pragmatic maxim and Dewey's deconstruction of the distinction between fine art and aesthetic criticism and the aesthetics of ordinary experience. As one seeks to anticipate consequences (Peirce), the question naturally arises: After conceivable outcomes are listed, even exhaustively, then what? Results are evaluated. But, how? In terms of the beauty, satisfaction, and fulfillment that they bring (Dewey). This might have the appearance of naive simplicity, but it is fiendishly complex and entangled. These chapters outline issues and problems that spin out primarily from two pragmatist texts, Peirce's pragmatic maxim (1905/1984) and Dewey's first chapter in *Art as Experience* (1934/1980).

CHAPTER 3

Meanings of Pragmatism and Pragmatic Meanings

For much of the twentieth century pragmatism was eclipsed in education, philosophy, the sciences, and the professions first by positivist and later by empiricist approaches to social thought and practice. Many believe (for example, see Rorty, 1967, 1979) that the renewed interest in pragmatism at the end of the century came about because positivism and empiricism had failed to produce the knowledge of the world that they had sought.[1] The possibility of attaining certain and positive knowledge by way of speaking correctly about the world had convincingly been called into question by the last three decades or so of the century (see Chapter 13 for a more extended discussion of these points).[2] Pragmatism offers an alternative. It turns away from true and correct speech to effective speech, to actions that bring with them desirable results.

Pragmatism and *praxis* are etymological descendants of the Greek *pragma*. Translations of *pragma* include "that which has been done," "a thing right or fit to be done," and "one's private affairs." *Pragma*, in turn, is related to the word *praggo*, that translates as "to achieve," "to bring about," "to accomplish," "to do," "to practice a way of life," and "to attend to." Putting these together, *pragmatism* points toward "acting," "living," "experiencing," and "doing." One meaning of *pragma* is "results of action."[3]

"Results of action" is strikingly close to the tenet that Charles Sanders Peirce outlined in what came to be known as the pragmatic maxim. Peirce initially stated the maxim, even though he did not use the word *pragmatism*, in his 1878 essay "How to Make Our Ideas Clear":

> Consider what effects which might conceivably have practical bearings we conceive the object of our conception to have, then, our conception of these effects is the whole of our conception of the object. (1878/1989, p. 88)

He offered this as a way of clarifying the meaning of intellectual concepts. He hoped that it would settle "metaphysical" disputes.[4] But Peirce's maxim is not altogether clear itself. It is fortunate, therefore, that Peirce took the opportunity to revise it in a 1905 essay review of a book on cosmology:

> The method prescribed in the [pragmatic] maxim is to trace out in the imagina-
> tion the conceivable practical consequences—the consequences for deliberate,
> self-controlled conduct—of the affirmation or denial of the concept; and the
> assertion of the maxim is that herein lies the *whole* of the purport of the word,
> the *entire* concept. (1905/1984, p. 494, emphasis in original)

Peirce initially promoted the pragmatic maxim as a way to clarify intellectual concepts. It is but a short step to extend the maxim to clarifying the
meaning of actions. If the pragmatist meaning of a concept rests in its
"conceivable practical consequences," then, by parallel argument, the
meaning of an action—say a policy such as bilingual education or a
classroom strategy such as cooperative learning—rests in its "conceivable
practical consequences" (see Chapters 7–11 for an extended example). The
difference between conceptualizing and acting distinguishes somewhat
between Peirce's interest in semiotics and William James's and John Dewey's interest in social policy.[5]

Lest I give the mistaken impression that thinking and acting are
structurally distinct, it should be pointed out that any distinction along
these lines quickly deconstructs. Thinking and imagining are themselves
actions. They result from material, physiological processes. But sometimes
it is important to focus on the act of thinking; at other times, on physical
actions. There is no rigid, clear-cut division between thought and action or,
in a more classical terminology, there is no firm mind/body distinction.[6]

Frank Macke, a contemporary pragmatist, gave the following broad
characterization of pragmatism, that arguably fuses thought and action.

> Any reflection on the meaning of pragmatism will inevitably remind us that
> *pragmatism is in essence a discourse on the consequences of thinking*. It is the self-
> consciousness of discourse: thinking aware of its own presence and history—
> discourse manifest to consciousness through the moments of its effect. (Macke,
> 1995, p. 158; emphasis added)

To be serious about conceivable consequences, following Peirce, requires
a discursive exploration of ideas. *Pragmatism* is used from time to time
to refer to "consequences," "results of action," and to "discourse[s] on
the consequences of thinking."

Where does one start in tracing conceivable practical consequences?
John Smith (1992) argued that Peirce rejected, "the idea that one 'must'
begin somewhere, since . . . one can only begin where one is—in the midst
of things and armed with a stock of beliefs that will retain their tenure

until there appears some critical reason for questioning them or replacing them with other beliefs" (p. 7). We begin with where we are—in context. The idea that we could begin tracing consequences from a "god's-eye view," one outside of context, is unavaible.

Pragmatism is very old and quite new. It is old in the sense that it is reasonable to believe that people have always been interested in the consequences of their beliefs and actions. Being interested in consequences surely has evolutionary survival value. In addition, it is likely that researchers of various denominations conduct research in order to understand consequences and the causes of consequences. Empirical researchers, for example, explore consequences conceptualized in terms of causal inferences by way of controlled and systematic inquiry. Interpretive researchers are interested in consequences that are associated with the way people differently understand and map their world. Critical researchers are concerned with the consequences produced by oppressive social relations as well as those that are generated when people secure enlightened self-understandings of how they have previously contributed to their own oppression.

Pragmatism is new in the sense that a "discourse on the consequences of thinking" exceeds the bounds of empiricist, interpretivist, critical, and other orthodoxies. Pragmatism does not name a doctrine. It is a fuzzy and ill-defined approach to thinking and living, for which it has been much criticized. It points, very generally, to ways of looking to the future.

CHAPTER 4

Pragmatism as a Term of Art

I was tempted to begin with Peirce's maxim and proceed chronologically. But others such as West (1989) and Thayer (1981) have done this, more or less, and done it well indeed. I begin with art and aesthetics, that, as John McDermott writes, "constitute the dramatic center of Dewey's philosophy" (1981, p. 525). Peirce's maxim implicitly poses a question: After imagining practical consequences, which consequences should we value and desire? I read Dewey's (1934/1980) argument in *Art as Experience* as answering that question. He tells us, in effect, that we should pursue aesthetically desirable consequences; pursue outcomes that are satisfying, fulfilling, harmonious, and beautiful; and explore what makes them so.

"Pragmatism is a term of art" (Margolis, 1986, p. 201). What can this mean?[1] The *OED* defines aesthetic as "things perceptible to the senses," "of or pertaining to the appreciation or criticism of the beautiful," and as a "philosophy or theory of taste, or of the perception of the beautiful in nature and art."[2] Although possibly at first a bit puzzling, the connection between pragmatism and art is quite straightforward. The argument can be briefly stated.

1. It is possible to generate a large and wide-ranging set of consequences if one traces the conceivable practical consequences of any idea.
2. Conceivable consequences are circumscribed by our experiences, our situation, the institutions within which we find ourselves, and the effects of power as it circulates in our subjectivities and interactions.
3. We can pursue some but not all imagined possibilities.
4. Therefore, pragmatists are constrained to choose among alternatives.
5. They behave as artists as they explore and exercise their imagination and desires through their choices.

The role and choices of an artist are forced upon pragmatists, as it were, when they conjecture about consequences, as is the role of art critic when these choices and productions are later evaluated. The pragmatic task of tracing conceivable consequences leads to questions about whether their conceptions, actions, and imagined consequences are in fact desirable, pleasurable, satisfying, and beautiful. Pragmatists are confronted and constrained by the limits of the world in which they find themselves, by what they can imagine. Artistic conceptions are sometimes ill defined, go through many revisions, change because of the particular array of resources at hand, and are applauded or faulted by others. But pragmatists would have us believe that we are all better off to the extent that we are better rather than lesser artists.

John Dewey addressed art and aesthetics at length in the ten William James Lectures that he gave at Harvard in 1931. They were later published as *Art as Experience* in 1934.[3] The argument Dewey developed seemingly inverts the title of his book from *Art as Experience* to *Experience as Art* because he deconstructed the accepted distinction between fine art and everyday life.[4] He wrote:

> A primary task is thus imposed upon one who undertakes to write upon the philosophy of the fine arts. This task is to restore continuity between the refined and intensified forms of experience that are works of art and the everyday events, doings, and sufferings that are universally recognized to constitute experience. (Dewey, 1934/1980, p. 3)

It would be difficult to emphasize the artistic in everyday experience more emphatically than Dewey did in the following passage:

> In order to *understand* the esthetic in its ultimate and approved forms, one must begin with it in the raw; in the events and scenes that hold the attentive eye and ear of man, arousing his interest and affording him enjoyment as he looks and listens: the sights that hold the crowd—the fire-engine rushing by; the machines excavating enormous holes in the earth; the human-fly climbing the steeple-side; the men perched high in air on girders, throwing and catching red-hot bolts. (1934/1980, pp. 4–5, emphasis in original)

> The intelligent mechanic engaged in his job, interested in doing well and finding satisfaction in his handiwork, caring for his materials and tools with genuine affection, is artistically engaged. (1934/1980, p. 5)

Aesthetic consequences and results of beliefs and actions are integral to ordinary experience, but in contemporary life, Dewey argues, the aesthetic has become elevated, detached, and alienated from its everyday origins.[5] Dewey wanted to recover "the continuity of esthetic experience with normal processes of living" (1934/1980, p. 10). He continued: "The esthetic is no intruder in experience from without;" instead, "it is the clarified and intensified development of traits that belong to every normally complete experience." (1934/1980, p. 46) Dewey (1934/1980) further characterized the aesthetic in these terms:

> Craftsmanship to be artistic in the final sense must be "loving"; it must care deeply for the subject matter upon which skill is exercised. (pp. 47–48)

> There is an element of passion in all esthetic perception. (p. 49)

> In as far as the development of an experience is *controlled* through reference to . . . [the] immediately felt relations of order and fulfillment, that experience becomes dominantly esthetic in nature. (p. 50, emphasis in original)

> The esthetic or undergoing phase of experience is receptive. It involves surrender. (p. 51)

> In a work of art . . . the end . . . is significant not by itself but as the integration of the parts. (p. 55)

The aesthetic is receptive, loving, passionate, holistic; it involves surrender, cares deeply, includes immediately felt relations of order and fulfillment, and is concerned with the integration of the parts. M. Regina Leffers gave this characterization of Dewey's aesthetics:

> In the doing phase of aesthetic experience, the quality of how we do what we do is at issue. Whether we are working on a professional paper, interacting with another human being, spending some time alone, or taking a brisk walk, the activity can be imbued with the *quality* of art, making it a "work of art." (1993, p. 72)

Richard Shusterman (1992) wrote a long and thoughtful commentary on and addendum to Dewey's conceptions of art and aesthetics:

> By . . . compartmentalizing art and the aesthetic as something to be enjoyed when we take a break from reality, the most hideous and oppressive institutions and practices of our civilization get legitimated and more deeply entrenched as inevitably real; they are erected as necessities to which art and beauty, by the reality principle must be subordinated. (p. 20)

There are no a priori reasons to exclude aesthetics from conceptions of practical consequences. There are practical reasons to assess aesthetically the results of our experiments in imagination and living.

Now transfer the aesthetic to the classroom. Some teachers, no doubt, would describe beautiful periods as those of shared quietness where everyone willingly and silently seeks to center themselves and bring focus to their thoughts, even if the words *centeredness* and *focus* are never used. Other teachers might report, to the contrary, episodes of high-energy, student-driven investigations when one hypothesis after another is tested. Some would be rejected, some not; the results would be used to generate further hypotheses and tests. Yet other teachers might identify lessons where students, as a result of the teacher's presentation (direct instruction), acquire collectively, and almost simultaneously, an insight into the nature of music, mathematics, or social relations.[6] Aesthetic pleasure is varied and it changes. But all teachers, students, and others who conceptualize consequences in the classroom take their turn at artistic production regardless of whether they think of themselves as artists.[7]

Thinking about consequences in terms of art and aesthetics may seem quite foreign and removed from the way we usually think about life, work, and society. But when I use the term *aesthetically desirable*, I use it to mean that I want things to turn out well. What does it mean for things to turn out well? Conceptions of wellness and well-being are continually constructed, deconstructed, and reconstructed. We may give different weights to various aesthetic characteristics at one point in time (a synchronic conception of wellness or well-being) and then change them in other times, places, and situations (a diachronic process). In education, for example, we may think of well-being in terms of high attendance and low vandalism, or high literacy rates and rich conceptions of literacy, or high scores on achievement and proficiency tests. These are competing aesthetic values that may or may not be positively correlated; how we interpret, combine, and trade them off defines, for the moment, our visions of beauty and desire.[8]

Now imagine a teacher who attempts to produce classroom beauty who is tempted, as a structuralist or empiricist might be, to draw a firm and lasting distinction between what is beautiful and what is not, what is fact and what is fiction, what is on-task and what is off-task. This temptation should be resisted.[9] Recall the examples above. In the first case, whereas student silence and centeredness may be beautiful in some contexts, in other settings such silence can inhibit spontaneous activity and oppose the decentering that is arguably necessary for moments of insight and interpretation (see Greene, 1972). In the second, student-centered inquiry may fail to take advantage of teacher expertise and, as a result, limit and reduce learning solely to students' newly constructed knowledge of the world (it might take some time to re-create quantum mechanics, for example). In the third, direct teaching, however beautiful and inspiring at its best, may diminish the ability of students to produce their own insights and texts. A beautiful/not-beautiful distinction deconstructs because what is beautiful is context-dependent. Contexts and purposes change. What is valued and disvalued are often reversed and reversed again. Actions that are beautiful in one setting may look ordinary and unremarkable in another. This is similar, for example, to a painting that was judged to be a masterpiece in the eighteenth century and now is seen to express an aesthetic vision that, although still appreciated by contemporary viewers, is prized primarily for its historical value. Likewise, as the context, critical frame, and values that one uses to assess classroom life vary, one's conception of beauty shifts and changes as well. This instability undermines a firm distinction between text (in this case a definition of beauty) and context (the situation in which the definition of beauty is applied). In tracing conceivable consequences we are well advised to attempt the impossible, to read the text-context entire.[10] Nor do I assume a distinction between art (the act of production) and aesthetics (the act of assessment and criticism) nor a distinction between tracing and assessing consequences. Each pair can certainly be spoken of separately, but they cannot be clearly distinguished.

This argument about art and aesthetics and pragmatism should not be interpreted as being dismissive of questions of ethics, science, politics, or other aspects of social life. Instead, the argument is that it is *within the context of aesthetics*, an aesthetics whose center endlessly recedes before us, that we project and explore constructions of ethics, knowledge, and justice. They jointly and interactively contribute to our sense of satisfaction and fulfillment. We are interested, I believe, in particular ethical systems, theories of justice, political ideologies, public policies, and beliefs that are accepted as true because of their aesthetic contributions to our lives. Do they bring us pleasure and satisfaction? Are they fulfilling?

Aesthetic values are unstable because they are dispersed and deferred. We continually interpret and criticize them. In education, control is desired sometimes, understanding sometimes, and emancipation from oppressive social relations at yet other times. But disaster is courted if one fixates upon a single and rigidly defined set of consequences and aesthetic values. The world surely changes whether our visions of beauty change or not. Pragmatist researchers, administrators, and teachers are artists and critics as they craft and subsequently criticize outcomes. Indeed pragmatism is a term of art where artistic conceptions and experiments remain moving targets. If one is interested in consequences, how could it be otherwise?

CHAPTER 5

Pragmatism as Effect and Cause of Knowledge and Power

Tracing conceivable practical consequences is a cognitive, social, and political as well as artistic exercise. Some things about tracing consequences are obvious. We begin imagining and speculating and hypothesizing from where we are. To do it well requires knowledge of self (who and where are we at the moment), problematic situation (uncertainty and the desire to reduce it), possible actions (what beliefs and tacks are feasible), potential outcomes from each action (cognitively mapping results, even though the map may be primitive), and estimating the value of the imagined consequences (comparing outcomes). These present obstacles and opportunities because self-conception, situation, possibility, potentiality, and value limit and open up our imagination.

From a phenomenological or interpretive view, our conceptions are restrained by what we are able to see. What we can see is conditioned by what we do see. And, what we see—in ourselves, others, the world—is shaped by who and where we are. This is one point of intersection among imagination, subjectivity, and power. Subjective conceptions of self, how we think about ourselves and act, come from observation and what one has undergone. Observation and experience, in their turn, feed back into and influence decisions about what to look at and how. Time and place and the exercise and effects of power, therefore, direct our gaze in ways that simultaneously circumscribes and generates possibilities about what we can conceive. Buried within Peirce's maxim, then, is the dynamic interaction of interpretation and power when one "trace[s] out in the imagination the conceivable practical consequences" of an intellectual concept or action. This, in turn, leads to pragmatism's need for wholesale criticism.

Research construes the world. Artistic motifs are elements of these construals, thereby linking art and cognition. Garrison's (1997, p. 92) discussion in *Dewey and Eros* pointed out that for Dewey, research and inquiry themselves are aesthetic endeavors. Dewey (1938/1986) wrote:

Inquiry is the controlled or directed transformation of an indeterminate situation into one that is so determinate in its constituent distinctions and relations as to convert the elements of the original situation into a unified whole. (p. 108)

Garrison (1997) further wrote that for Dewey "Inquiry . . . serves practical interests" (p. 88) and "the purpose of inquiry is not . . . to discover timeless truths. Rather inquiry seeks to arrive temporarily at 'warranted assertions' that aid in transforming the environment so that humanity may maintain and enjoy its precarious existence" (pp. 90–91). Emphasizing practical interests and disavowing "timeless truths" means that inquiry is an ongoing interpretation of the world. As Garrison observed, *eros, poesis,* and *techne* merge (see Garrison, 1997, Chapter 4).

If research construes the world, it is also the case that we inherit research traditions that selectively champion some construals over others—the traditions we inherit can be said to have evolutionary survival value in some sense. Survival—recall the previous chapter—surely has aesthetic appeal. Embedded in different research traditions, if Dewey and Garrison are correct (and I think that they are), are visions of what is beautiful and desirable. It does not seem possible to disentangle these visions from the skills that are required to produce them. This is similar to the way a painter's vision is limited by the materials at hand—canvas, frame, paints, brushes, and, of course, imagination (this is another way to deny an ends/means distinction). Each research-generated construction of the world, furthermore, finds expression at the expense of alternative views that were rejected. This is because we cannot simultaneously describe and explain the world from all standpoints, from a "god's-eye view." It is arguably the case that much of the contentiousness among adherents of different approaches to inquiry and research is about aesthetic values as much as it is about the production of statements that function as true. Empiricist (quantitative, experimental, quasi-experimental), interpretivist (qualitative, ethnographic, field), and critical research methodologies, to mention three of the more widely known and contested approaches to educational research, each has a particular aesthetic orientation. If inquiry and practical reasoning begin with desire (see Garrison, 1997, p. xviii), then the constructions produced by research respond to that desire. Here is a brief sketch, exceedingly so, of some of the aesthetic values that are complicit with alternative approaches to inquiry.

A major goal of empiricist research, the dominant and most widely practiced approach to educational research, is to document plausibly causal relationships. These can be between, for example, teaching strategies and student behaviors. A knowledge of specific causal relationships, this well-rehearsed argument goes, enables one to introduce planned intercessions in administrative or classroom practices. Empiricist research and the subsequent policy planning and implementations that are premised upon it highlight the aesthetic values of control, efficiency, productivity, and rational planning. The aesthetic appeals of empiricist research findings are rooted in promises of reliability. If cause and effect can be reliably reported and reproduced, then the likelihood of unknown and unwanted outcomes is diminished and the likelihood of desired consequences is enhanced. Now consider the aesthetic dimensions related to interpretivist and critical research.[1] One goal of interpretive research is to document how individuals understand themselves, their surroundings, and their situations. How do subjects make sense of the world? Interpretive research aims to produce understanding instead of causal relationships. Individuals who are objects of empirical research are subjects in interpretive research. Instead of being asked questions predetermined by a researcher, to tell a story that has previously been outlined in the hypotheses of the researcher, individuals are asked to tell a story of the world as they see it. Understanding, in turn, promotes communication, tolerance, and acceptance. Interpretive knowledge, as a result, increases our ability to imagine ourselves from the perspectives of others. The aesthetic values that are underscored and reinforced by interpretive knowledge include not only self and mutual understanding but also meaningful communication, affiliation, and connection. These values contrast sharply with those of empiricism, because an aesthetics of control is far down any list of interpretive values.

Critical researchers prize yet a different set of aesthetic values. They emphasize that the effects of power operate through their own research as well as in schools and other research sites. One result of the exercise and effect of power is that some individuals and groups—such as women, people of color, and those who are impoverished—are, if not silenced and disenfranchised by our educational practices, nudged, shoved, and cast to the margins. Critical researchers seek to counter the social practices that produce marginalization and subjugation by educating and enlightening those who unwittingly participate in their own oppression. When those who are oppressed understand how they contribute to their own oppression, the argument of critical theorists goes, they will be better equipped to resist collaborating in their own domination. The aesthetic values of critical research embrace enlightenment, emancipation, and agency in contrast to the empiricist's emphasis on control and the interpretivist's commitment to understanding. Whatever paradigm wars we witness, I believe, are about aesthetic choices as much as about which statements we choose to function as true. Research goals such as certainty and control, understanding and communication, and enlightenment and emancipation can easily be cast in aesthetic terms. Doing so contributes to the deconstruction of an aesthetic/cognitive distinction.

Peirce's pragmatic maxim, as previously observed, is concerned with meanings. Meanings are social constructs. Why? Because they are consequences of thinking. The word *construct*, it should be noted, is structurally ambiguous. It is both noun and verb. It names what is constructed and points to the act of construction. Putting the two usages together provides another bridge between aesthetics and cognition. As aesthetically desirable consequences are constructed, they point to the cognitive processes and conditions of their construction.

From where do our conceptions of consequences come? Here is a short answer: Conceivable practical consequences are socially constructed within contexts that are political, economic, cultural, ethnic, socially stratified, linguistically diverse, and gendered.[2] They are produced by individuals interacting with others. Power and ideology, as well as intellectual traditions, operate to produce and reproduce the social institutions and processes within which meanings are constructed and assessed.[3] The exercise and effects of power, whereby some people are indulged and others are deprived, in institutional as well as idiosyncratic settings, shape the social construction of meanings.

How might this work? In one well-known formulation, Dahl (1957) conceptualized power as a relation among people or groups whereby one person or group has power to the extent they are able to extract otherwise unforthcoming behavior from another. Foucault (see Dreyfus & Rabinow, 1983, p. 185), in contrast, thought of power as circulating in the micropractices of a profession or society. By combining these views, power can be thought of as circulating in unequal transactions between parties. As individuals move from one setting or institution to another, their relative position of being advantaged or disadvantaged changes. Some person or group who has more power in one setting frequently will have less in another.

Foucault's (1980b) conception of decentered power links pragmatism to the social construction of consequences.

There is no power that is exercised without a series of aims and objectives. But this does not mean that it results from the choice or decision of an individual subject; let us not look for the headquarters that presides over its rationality. . . . It is often the case that no one is there to have invented them [the rationality of power and its tactics], and few who can be said to have formulated them. (p. 95)

Foucault (1980b) took the argument another step when he wrote that

> We should try to discover how it is that subjects are gradually, progressively, really and materially constituted through a multiplicity of organisms, forces, energies, materials, desires, thoughts, etc. We should try to grasp subjection in its material instance and a constitution of subjects. (p. 97)[4]

This presents pragmatists with a complicating problem. Our conceptions of consequences and their assessment, it seems, exist before we think them. We inherit preexisting conceptions, desires, and methodologies that we use to trace outcomes. A person's subjectivity, how an individual thinks about herself and behaves, is a social construction that includes beliefs, desires, conceptions of beauty, and cognitive strategies. The constructed self itself is an outcome. It produces subsequent generations of constructions. Thus the constructions that combine to form our subjective conceptions beget more constructions and on and on.

If pragmatism is a discourse on the consequences of thinking, it is a discourse that narrates a complicated dance between aesthetics and power, and knowledge and power, and aesthetics and knowledge, and all at once. Pragmatists seek aesthetically desirable meanings; they want things to turn out well, as they trace conceivable practical consequences in the context of power, ideology, and history. It is possible, they understand, that what appears to be a freely chosen aesthetic or a rationally calculated outcome may well be a highly determined effect of power and ideology. *Aesthetic conceptions and desires are generated in unequal social transactions.* Therefore, revealing and criticizing power is required if one is seriously interested in conceptualizing consequences. If pragmatism is a dance among aesthetics, knowledge, and power, then power operates to prohibit some movements, steps, and tempos while encouraging others.

Knowledge of consequences is textual. Power generates text. Pragmatists produce texts when thinking about outcomes. What is text? Among the usages given in the *OED* are: "the wording of anything written or printed; the structure formed by the words in their order; the very words, phrases, and sentences as written" and "the theme or subject on which any one speaks; the starting point of a discussion; a statement on which any one dilates." I use *text* in both ways. Sometimes text is employed as "the wording of anything written or printed" and sometimes as "the theme or subject on which any one speaks." In the latter case, one can speak of all the world as text. When these two views of text are combined in the quest for consequences, the pragmatist task becomes the construction of text (conceivable consequences) upon text (the object of our conjectures). Silverman (1994) wrote:

> The text . . . is not the work. The work . . . is a fragment of substance, occupying a part of the space of books (in a library for example). The text is a methodological field. . . . When the author returns to the text, it is as a guest. The text is plural; its multiple meanings are neither centered nor closed off. . . . Text . . . is located where language opens up a horizon of interpretive meaning. . . . The text is an open system of signs with plural meanings. (pp. 29–30)

Pragmatists are in the business of sorting through the texts with which they come in contact while generating texts designed to produce more desirable and beautiful outcomes.

Subjecting texts and interpretations to criticism begins, even if completion is not contemplated, a discourse about whether or not they are accurate, pleasing, productive, efficient, or persuasive or some or all of these and more. Criticism can be by way of logical argument, moral debate, and empirical investigation, among others. The word *criticism*, again from the *OED*, refers to "the action of . . . passing judgement upon the qualities or merits of anything." Pragmatism requires criticism about the value of desires and consequences, the production of anticipated consequences, and the circumstances that surround their production.

Scholars such as Michel Foucault (1973, 1980a, 1980b) and Jurgen Habermas (1976, 1979), among others, offer important insights for pragmatists. They forcefully argued that the (1) material and social arrangements within which we (2) formulate images of the future (3) cannot be sharply distinguished from each other. Foucault observed that "critique doesn't have to be the premise of a deduction that concludes: This then is what needs to be done. It should be an instrument for those who fight, those who resist and refuse what is" (1980/1991, p. 80). This comment speaks to pragmatism, in which criticism is aesthetic and artistic as well as intellectual and political. Social and political inequalities are likely to be with us forever. They are obvious targets for pragmatist scrutiny.

CHAPTER 6

Pragmatism as a Democratic, Inductive, and Anti-Essentialist Experiment

Pragmatism requires democracy.[1] There is conspicuous value in drawing on multiple conjectures, speculations, descriptions, and interpretations when conceptualizing consequences. This is a particularly strong example of how text (imagined consequences) is dependent on context (situation, setting).[2] Social openness, inclusiveness, tolerance, and experimentation generate more outcomes than closed, exclusive, and intolerant deliberations. This is because despotism, autocracy, authoritarianism, and rigidity inhibit free-flowing conversations and discourse.

Seigfried (1993) emphasized this point when she brought the insights of feminism and pragmatism together: "A central problem investigated by pragmatists over the years is how to preserve diversity in unity and how to develop unity out of diversity" (p. 2). She continued:

> Pragmatism naturalized the transcendental search for eternal truths about reality by reflecting on the various ways that members of a community come to agree on the explanations that best join the funded character of experience with the goals sought and then critically revise their conclusions in light of further developments. (p. 2)

Gregory Pappas, commenting on Dewey, wrote that "ethical inquiry needs to start with experience as one finds it. What one finds in more experience is interaction and not the traditional picture of an isolated moral conscience with duties and desires as her possessions" (1993, p. 88). Thomas Alexander (1995) set these ideas in a larger context: "Democracy cannot merely 'tolerate' diversity; it alone of all forms of civilization *requires* diversity. . . . There is an initial need to *encounter difference meaningfully*" (pp. 75–76, emphasis in original).

Here is one argument that links democracy and pragmatism:

1. There are no guarantees that the individual conceptions (actions) that we are disposed to affirm or deny (enact or avoid) are accurate or beautiful or effective (are productive or lead to the outcomes we desire).
2. Without conclusive evidence about the consequences and outcomes of our ideas and actions, it is reasonable (rational) to explore a wide variety of conceptions (courses of action) because it is possible that someone else might have more accurate or beautiful or affective ideas.
3. Efficient and open communication among individuals and groups enhances the review of possible outcomes.
4. Authoritarian, hierarchical, and traditional organizations and relationships—in general, those that demand ideological or programmatic purity—limit the consequences that can be imagined (such organizations are not pragmatic, nor is that their aim).
5. Pragmatism and democracy are allies because pragmatism requires the openness that democracy provides and pragmatism encourages the experimentation that constitutes democracy.

Robert Westbrook (1991) quoted Dewey on this point: There can be no dispute about a "socialism of the intelligence and of the spirit. To extend the range and the fullness of sharing in the intellectual and spiritual resources of the community is the very meaning of community" (p. 94). Democracies are experimental. Experiments are problematic. This brings us to fallibilism.

Pragmatism is fallibilistic, contextual, contingent, and holistic.[3] I discuss these in turn—first, fallibilism. A discourse on the consequences of thinking always courts unanticipated or unappealing outcomes or both; we run the risk that our conjectures will be wrong, and sometimes being wrong can be dangerous. We can be mistaken, for example, about the desirability of our aesthetic tastes, knowledge of the world, and trustworthiness of social and political institutions. The source of the problem is that imagining consequences is an inductive process. Art and aesthetics, knowledge and research, public policy and policy outcomes, classroom strategies and their effects—experiences all, as Dewey might put it—are inductive enterprises. Discourse on thinking and experience continually moves from where we are to where we are not, from what is known to what is unknown.

Here is a brief review of the inductive problem that leads to pragmatist fallibilism:

A1. All observed Xs (say, mastery learning interventions) have been Ys (say, followed by improved standardized achievement scores).

B. Therefore, all future Xs (mastery learning interventions) will be Ys
   (followed by improved standardized achievement scores).

As with all inductive arguments, the premise (A1) can be true and the
conclusion (B) false. This is because the conclusion (B) contains information (the results of future mastery learning interventions) that is absent
from the premise (A1) (Salmon, 1963, pp. 14–17). The problem of turning
A1 and B into a valid and truth-preserving argument is easily solved by
the addition of a second premise.

A1. All observed Xs (mastery learning interventions) have been Ys (fol-
    lowed by improved standardized achievement scores).
A2. The future will be like the past.
B. Therefore, all future Xs (mastery learning interventions) will be Ys
    (followed by improved standardized achievement scores).

The addition of A2 turns a fallible inductive argument into a valid deductive argument in which the conclusion preserves whatever truth resides
in its premises. It may be a valid and truth-preserving argument, but
practically it is useless. To make it a valid argument, we must assume
what we do not know, that the future will be like the past. Speculation
about the future, about which we cannot have determinate knowledge,
is what is at stake in conceptualizing consequences of beliefs and actions.
Pragmatists are interested in whether the future will be like the past, to
be sure. But they along with everyone else must act before the fact, before
the future reveals itself.
    Fallibilism is usually thought of as a characteristic of cognitive induc-
tive predictions. For example, is it possible to predict the effect of combining whole language and phonics? But artistic conceptions and aesthetic
values are also inductive activities. They predict what will and will not
bring satisfaction and pleasure. We can be as easily mistaken about artistic
consequences as about the reading scores that whole-language and phonics instruction will produce. Here is how Shusterman (1992) put it: "Our
aesthetic concepts, including the concept of art itself, are but instruments
which need to be challenged and revised when they fail to provide the
best experience" (p. 18). What constitutes the best experience, however,
is a question that is also continually deferred. However superb our outcomes and experience, there is always the possibility that something better
will come along or that what we will change our mind about what we
want or what is beautiful. Tomorrow is another day. Even when we firmly
believe in the importance of a social value, such as social equality, we
should not be surprised if what social equality means is reinterpreted

from situation to situation and time to time or sometimes requires social inequality.

Second, contextualism. Contexts, the settings and situations that constitute the possibility of our texts, change. Confidence about how things work in one situation is often problematic in another (another form of the problem of induction). At the risk of stating the obvious, two situations must be different in at least one way or they are the same situation. Therefore, knowledge of results from one lesson or activity or unit, for example, cannot be applied with full confidence at a later time even in the same classroom or school. With the passage of time, one situation becomes two (an illustration of Derrida's *differance*). In the literature on research design, this is known as the problem of external validity (Cook & Campbell, 1979). Different situations are, by definition, different. The interaction of text with context never ends.[4]

Third, contingency. The *OED* defines contingent as "not determined by necessity in regard to action or existence: free." There is no assurance, what could it be or where would it come from, that the world is constant, stable, or in some form of stasis. Speculation and experimentation are circumscribed by the contingency of the world. Imagine fallibility, context, and contingency operative in the classroom. Teachers have ideas. They present them in an orderly fashion. These are texts that the teacher enacts. They can be deliberately and deliberatively penned in unit and lesson plans. And they work splendidly first time through. Confronted with different students, say a year later, the lessons will likely work better or worse but differently. The two groups of students will likely read the text of the teacher's presentation differently.

Fourth, holism. When we give up the text/context distinction, we deny ourselves the luxury of looking at the world in fragments. Looking to results and consequences cannot be categorically limited, except by stipulation, before the fact. Culture or politics or other complicating factors cannot be bracketed out. One effect of fallibilism, contextualism, and contingency is that they lead us to evade, to use West's (1989) term, dualisms such as fact/value, objective/subjective, rational/irrational, analytic/synthetic, scheme/content, theory/practice, ends/means, description/prescription, and logic/rhetoric that have long characterized modern, analytic, and scientific thought.[5]

Feminism and pragmatism share a holistic attitude. Mary Leach (1995) wrote that

> Dualisms of the kind feminists are busy deconstructing, (subject-object, mind-body, consciousness-matter, each separate from each other and wholly independent) are, we would argue, reflective *products*, secondary objects *mistaken*

for genuinely primary experience (diversity and identity, inter-connections and gaps, change and permanence, instability and stability, interdependent natural objects and organisms of all kinds, including the human organism). (p. 299, emphasis in original)

Abandoning binary distinctions also captures affinities that pragmatism shares with poststructuralism. Rorty wrote that "pragmatists and Derrideans are, indeed, natural allies. Their strategies supplement each other admirably" (1985, p. 135). We are led by this reasoning to use the logic of structuralist planning, policy, and teaching when it produces outcomes we would otherwise desire, but not because of their "essential" properties (see Cherryholmes, 1988, for a longer discussion of this issue in education).

The problem of inductive inference forces the four preceding positions upon pragmatists. It also disabuses them of the pretenses of essentialism, representationalism, and foundationalism, to which I now turn.[6] Pragmatists reject these three positions because they have no wish to "get things right." Nor do they think it is possible to do so. To be more precise, because pragmatists are fallibilists, they are agnostic rather than atheistic on these issues. Why? Because their fallibility could extend to essentialist, representationalist, and foundationalist beliefs. Positivists, empiricists, and phenomenologists seek to speak *correctly* about the world, albeit each employs different assumptions and methodologies. Pragmatists wish to speak and act *effectively* in the world.

Essentialism is "a metaphysical theory that objects [such as rocks, photons, textbooks, and standardized assessment tests] have essences and that there is a distinction between essential and non-essential or accidental predications" (Loux, 1996, p. 241). It is the task of researchers, in this view, to "get things right" by determining what is essentially going on. But human knowledge and the estimation of consequences result from human activity. It is possible to describe and interpret any event and object in as many ways as there are describers and interpreters. A critic might argue that this opens the door for chaos, anarchy, and a radical cognitive relativism whereby every belief and taste is of equal worth. But to give up the search for a final and determinate "Truth" does not concede that all beliefs are equally valuable. If you are interested in consequences, you are an unqualified realist. It is not possible to treat all beliefs as equally valid.

Essentialists are at a disadvantage because they do not have benchmarks against which to test their descriptions and interpretations. For example, how could anyone know that they have seen and reported an essence or gotten closer to or farther away from one? People have different purposes when they trace out conceivable practical consequences as opposed to a "god's-eye view." Different purposes should often produce different projections and evaluations of the same concept, action, or outcome. They may be equally accurate yet be contradictory (see Part III for an extended example).

Once essentialism goes, representationalism follows. Rorty (1979) describes representational knowledge as: "To know is to represent accurately what is outside the mind; so to understand the possibility and nature of knowledge is to understand the way in which the mind is able to construct such representations" (p. 3). If there is no essence of, say, intelligence or classroom climate or higher-order thinking, then it is a mistake to believe that this thing that has no essence can be "accurately" and "objectively" re-presented. Rorty (1990) wrote:

> It is useless to ask whether one vocabulary rather than another is closer to reality. For different vocabularies serve different purposes, and there is no such thing as a purpose that is closer to reality than another purpose. In particular, there is no purpose that is simply "finding out how things are" as opposed to finding out how to predict their motion, explain their behavior, and so on. (p. 3)

Does nature have a purpose? If nature had a purpose how would we know if our purposes matched it?

Foundationalism, as discussed here, is the "thesis that criteria of justification are not purely conventional but stand in the need of objective grounding, being satisfactory only if truth-indicative," (Haack, 1993, p. 130).[7] This is an immensely ambitious idea. As argued above, if events and objects lack essences, then we must forgo the goal of definitively representing them. As a result, there is little (no) hope that foundational rules can be constructed that will detect when representations are true or false by capturing some essential character of an event or object. We are left with reliability. This may not be exciting, but it is useful.

Pragmatists do not choose explanations or theories because they are better "representations" or "conceptions" or "pictures" of "reality," of what is really "real." We get insights into whether our beliefs work or not by acting on them and observing the consequences. These are tests that could yield contrary results on the occasion of a future test. Opponents of pragmatism who advocate essentialism, representationalism, or foundationalism of one sort or another are in the unenviable position of invoking nonpragmatic or post-pragmatic criteria for success. Such opponents must appeal to something beyond results and consequences if they are to separate themselves from pragmatism. A foundationalist or pre-pragmatic or post-pragmatic project that lies beyond consequences is difficult to imagine. How does one get beyond the texts of our observations? How can one transcend the interpretation, criticism, and revision of these texts? Pragmatists appreciate the successes and victories of modern science and technology without question. Modern science and technology has been *effective* in producing desired results. Pragmatists reject interpretations of the persuasive and effective stories of science, its successes, as foundational knowledge. Sometime in the future, say 200 or 300 years from now, if not next week, someone may discover and conclusively demonstrate that events and things have essences and in the process specify the foundational rules to follow in representing them truly and correctly. "Do not block the road to inquiry" has been a pragmatist tenet since Peirce's maxim, from the time the first pragmatist conceptualized the construction of meaning as the outcome of an inductive experiment.

Critics of this reading of pragmatism or of pragmatism itself sometimes argue that all social theorists and practitioners are interested in the consequences of thinking and acting. Here is one such argument:

1. Pragmatism is a discourse on the consequences of thinking;
2. all social theorists and practitioners are interested in the consequences of thinking; therefore,
3. if pragmatism is everything when it comes to social theory, then there is nothing distinctive about it, and
4. if there is nothing distinctive about pragmatism, it cannot be linked to a particular politics.

There are two criticisms here. First, pragmatism lacks distinctiveness. Second, it cannot be linked to a particular politics, say a democratic politics. This issue was the point of an exchange between Ernesto Laclau and Rorty. Here is how Laclau (1996) put a more restrictive and sophisticated version of this attack on pragmatism:

> If pragmatic redescription is all there has been in history—and I do not back down from this conclusion—Rorty [and other pragmatists have] . . . to show in what way not only Dewey, James or Wittgenstein have been engaged in pragmatic games, but also all kind of metaphysicians and dogmatic politicians who claimed to be doing exactly the opposite. Pragmatism becomes, in that way, something like an intellectual horizon allowing us to describe all currents of thought and all events in history. In that case, however, we cannot derive from pragmatistic premises any particular politics [such as democratic politics]. (p. 61)

Richard Rorty (1996) responded:

> I do *not* 'want to ground on pragmatist premises the concrete politics' I advocate, nor do I think that today's liberalism is 'the moment of full aware-

ness of what is involved in pragmatism.' . . . Do I . . . try to weld my liberalism and my pragmatism? Only to the following extent: I think that both are the expressions of, and reinforce, the same sort of suspicions of religion and metaphysics. Both can be traced back to some of the same historical causes (religious tolerance, constitutional democracy, Darwin). This is not a very tight weld, but I am not interested in making it any tighter. (pp. 73–74, emphasis in original)

It may or may not be the case that "pragmatic redescription is all there has been in history." Laclau (1996) also put it like this: "Pragmatism becomes . . . something like an intellectual horizon allowing us to describe all currents of thought and all events in history" (p. 61). But intellectual horizons, as with geographical horizons, are not identical. Some geographical horizons are determined by the sea, by ice, by mountain tops, by desert views, by rolling plains, by skyscrapers, and on and on. Some intellectual horizons are determined by structural assertions, by textual assumptions, by foundational principles of justice, epistemology, aesthetics, ethics, and, in the case of pragmatism, by a discourse on the consequences of thinking. These intellectual horizons provide the backdrop for a seemingly interminable array of redescriptions of the world.

Pragmatism's distinctive intellectual horizon forgoes first and final principles and abjures distinctions between text and context, fact and value, subject and object, analytic and synthetic, and theory and practice. It does not produce a unique reading of history, society, or education. There arguably are feminist (Fraser, 1989), meliorist (Campbell, 1992), speculative (Rosenthal, 1990), prophetic (West, 1989), deconstructionist (Derrida, 1996), liberal (Rorty, 1982), aesthetic (Shusterman, 1992), and democratic (Dewey, 1934/1980) pragmatists, at least. Each proposes a way to tell stories about unknown consequences.

Must a pragmatic politics be democratic or liberal? Here, again, Laclau (1996) puts the question to pragmatism and deconstruction:

The question that looms on the horizon is this: are we really *applying* deconstruction and pragmatism to the political field or, rather, by radicalizing their respective logics are we unveiling their ultimately political nature? (p. 67, emphasis in original)

We do both. A discourse on the consequences of thinking necessarily leads to politics. The discourse is necessarily political, and it is a democratic politics. Pragmatists as a matter of course look to deconstruct the putative political/nonpolitical distinction that Laclau suggests.

This reading of pragmatism has outlined its value for an individual pragmatist and those who are like-minded. But there is always the possibility that a pragmatist will encounter a dogmatist and ideologue. What to do? The dogmatist, for purposes of argument, is likely to be an essentialist, representationalist, or foundationalist, a fundamentalist at heart. Obviously, this "other" can break off communication and insist on rigid adherence to first principles in an effort to "get things right." Even though this limits the options for a pragmatist, several strategies are available in such an imaginary encounter. First, continue the conversation. Conversations can be educational. Education was important to Dewey's pragmatism for good reason. Second, highlight the role of interpretation in social life. Even fundamentalists are required to interpret their revealed texts. Disagreements about revelation, whether sacred or secular, are evidence that interpretations are problematic. Third, emphasize that degrees of freedom are interpretively available and that some of this freedom can be used to promote beauty, satisfaction, and fulfillment. Interpretations can advance aesthetically pleasing outcomes. Fourth, note that criticism can be useful not only in policing outcomes, as an ideologue might, but in enriching them.[8]

The point of such a conversation is to persuade the dogmatist to make the linguistic turn—and this does not deny external realities or external world. Language is very important in coping with and negotiating our way in the world. Its malleability, fluidity, and ambiguity (see Chapter 13 for a detailed argument along these lines) require interpretation and criticism of interpretations. Once language is de-reified, then fundamentalist arguments and positions become less attractive. They certainly become more vulnerable. It is likely, however, that there will be dogmatists who resist these efforts at conversion and reject the linguistic turn.

READING RESEARCH: CONSEQUENCES AND THE CONSTRUCTION OF MEANING

At first, Peirce's maxim appears to be straightforward and uncomplicated. But anticipating practical consequences turns out, as indicated in Parts I and II, to be remarkably involved. To demonstrate some of this complexity, an extended example of imagining practical consequences is developed in Part III. The consequences that are investigated come from affirming the findings of a well-known and widely cited research study of reciprocal teaching (Palincsar & Brown, 1984). Consequences of the research are separately constructed from feminist, critical, and deconstructive perspectives. This pragmatist exercise provides an opportunity to explore the divergence and convergence of pragmatic meanings from statements that operate as true. If pragmatism ever seemed simple, the simplisms evaporate when confronted with difference. I pose two questions for the next few chapters: What does it practically mean to read research for its conceivable consequences (following Peirce's maxim)? What does it mean to discuss and deliberate conflicts among consequences that are conceivable (exploring Macke's "discourse on the consequences of thinking")?

CHAPTER 7

Another Problem of Reading

This reading of pragmatism may provoke more questions than it answers. Some problematic issues, for example, were bypassed when the previous arguments about art, aesthetics, knowledge, power, fallibilism, and anti-essentialism were developed in Part II. Now, I take up the practical problem that the same concept or action means different things to different people. A closely related issue is that pragmatic meanings and statements that operate as true converge and diverge depending on purpose and context. My use of pragmatic meaning continues to come straight from Peirce's maxim, where meaning is the "trac[ing] out in the imagination the conceivable practical consequences . . . of the affirmation or denial of . . . [a] concept." I contrast such meanings to statements that function as true. I agree with Lynn Nelson (1993) when she recalled Dewey's argument that we make intellectual progress more by getting past questions than by answering them. She wrote: "'What is Truth'? is such a question (though 'What is true?' is not)" (p. 173). When I use the term *true* I mean, no more and no less than, what it is reasonable to believe under the circumstances.[1] What is true, then, is colloquial and context-dependent (this is not far removed from Dewey's characterization of truth as warranted assertability).[2] This is not a robust conception, to say the least. Here is how Rorty (1982) expresses this idea:

> People have, oddly enough, found something interesting to say about the essence of Force and the definition of "number." They might have found something interesting to say about the essence of Truth. But in fact they haven't. . . . When . . . [pragmatists] suggest that we not ask questions about the nature of Truth and Goodness, they do not invoke a theory about the nature of reality or knowledge or man which says that "there is no such thing" as Truth or Goodness. Nor do they have a "relativistic" or "subjectivistic" theory of Truth or Goodness. They would simply like to change the subject. (p. xiv)

"Changing the subject" is consequential. It involves a turn, if you will, *from* reading research findings as correct statements about the world (as a positivist or empiricist or field researcher might) *to* reading research

findings for their effectiveness in plotting conceivable practical consequences.

Researchers read research? They are experienced readers, to be sure.
They have read textbook after textbook as undergraduate and graduate
students, they have read the text of the setting within which they conduct
research, and they have read the research of others. But it is arguable that
conventional readings that seek the facts of the matter—say, empiricist
readings that are shaped by methodological guidelines learned in research
seminars—display as much naivete as sophistication. The characteristics
of a sophisticated empiricist reading have been well rehearsed and are
widely known. Researchers read to find generalizations for which empirical support has been collected. They read to assess evidence for and
against hypotheses. They read to detect theoretical and empirical inconsistencies and gaps. But empiricist and theoretical readings do not exhaust
the possibilities of reading research. There are many ways to read, interpret, and criticize. Some include attending to subtexts about gender; criticisms of social oppression; rhetorical and logical coherence; metaphor,
synecdoche, and other literary tropes; and textual structures.

Naive readings are deficient in informed judgment. This can perhaps
be said of all readings. To say that all are naive does not to deny that
there are variations in degree and standpoint. Researchers, for example,
who were trained in empiricist techniques might display a lack of informed judgment by restricting themselves to technical issues. The silence
of the empiricist research literature on the textuality of research findings,
reports, books, monographs, articles, and conference papers seems to
presuppose two things. First, that those who study research methodology
and conduct research already are expert readers. Second, that if one is
skilled in research design, data collection, data analysis, hypothesis test-
ing, and so on, one is pointed in the right direction when reading research.
Key questions for those schooled in the research traditions portrayed in
leading textbooks focus on reading in terms of whether the sample was
appropriately selected, whether the measurements were reliable and
valid, whether the correct statistical analyses were conducted, and
whether the assumptions of the statistical tests were satisfied?

I pose a post-empiricist question, one that comes after the research
is completed. After we are satisfied on the point of what it is most reasonable to believe under the circumstances, if it is possible to so agree, how
do we determine what such truths mean. This is the pragmatist question.
Truths and meanings are both constructions. They are produced in contexts where power and images of beauty and satisfaction endlessly circulate. Here is part of the argument: (1) The distinction between truths and
meanings deconstructs; (2) even if we can agree upon which statements

are to function as true, their meanings are dispersed; (3) therefore, we choose among dispersed meanings on the basis of satisfaction and fulfillment (authoritarians dictate what is beautiful, democrats and pragmatists negotiate what is beautiful). This points to what is literary and artistic in educational research and the social sciences.

Richard Rorty (1982) boldly states this complex construction, deconstruction, and blending of truth and meaning:

> If we get rid of traditional notions of "objectivity" and "scientific method" we shall be able to see the social sciences as continuous with literature—as interpreting other people to us, and thus enlarging and deepening our sense of community. (p. 203)[3]

The belief that the social sciences are continuous with literature may appear heretical. It certainly is at odds with dominant dogmas. Complex research designs, ingenuous measuring instruments, involved statistical analyses, and formal mathematical models seem to have little in common with the stories that novelists tell or the images that poets invoke. If the social sciences are continuous with literature, if what operates as true is continuous with pragmatist meaning, it is incumbent upon those who believe these things to explain these continuities and what difference they make. Pragmatists must answer pragmatic questions.

Research findings tell stories. Often, they are about putative causes and effects. Sometimes they are descriptive, sometimes explanatory. Research findings tell stories that are, more or less, insightful and useful in shaping what we think and do. The continuity-with-literature argument does not allege that social scientific research findings are another form of poetry or that they are structured like short stories or novels (see J. Nelson, Megill, & McCloskey, 1987, for an introduction to rhetorical analyses of the social sciences). They are useful in helping us to understand our social world as we navigate our way through it. But how are we to read the genre that we call research?

FOUNDATIONALISM REVISITED

It is useful to revisit the issue of foundationalism that is here called fundamentalism—no religious connotation intended. Robert Scholes (1989) discussed and criticized a fundamentalist approach to reading that roughly parallels what some who would support a foundationalist approach might advocate:

Textual fundamentalism is the belief that texts always say just what they mean, so that any honest or decent person ought to be able to understand this perfectly clear meaning without making any fuss about it. . . . The fundamentalist view of interpretation requires two things: that meaning be fixed eternally, outside of time, and that texts in time-bound languages convey that meaning so directly that it can be discerned without interpretation. Fundamentalist attempts to fix the meaning of texts all—without exception—can be shown to require some timeless zone in which true meanings are said to reside. (pp. 52–53)

In the context of reading research, a fundamentalist reader would require that the meaning of an observation be "fixed eternally, outside of time" and that the "time-bound languages" of research— for example, statistical, mathematical, verbal, or computer—"convey that meaning so directly that it can be discerned without interpretation." Such a fundamentalist approach to reading must be scrapped because even if would-be positivists or empiricists were inclined toward this theory of reading, they, as well as the rest of us, are denied a language "outside or time" that requires no interpretation.

Deprived of foundational principles, how are we to read? In the next few chapters an extended pragmatist exercise in reading a research finding is advanced. It seeks to clarify meanings with an eye toward consequences, even though the meanings may turn out to be elusive. It will become clear that while facts about objects and events are one thing, what they mean is something else. Pragmatist readers emphatically reject the idea that facts or narrative plots or theories or metaphors or statistical explanations or formal models ever speak for themselves. They also reject the contention that texts have but one meaning.

Reading research to clarify meanings does not promise agreement or consensus. It should be noted from the outset that reading pragmatically, reading to clarify meanings, does not refer to reading merely with an eye to problem solving or for short run instrumental gain or for purposes of economic or social efficiency (see Cherryholmes, 1988, Chapter 8). Empirical researchers often seem to search for and attempt to produce texts that "get things right," express truth, or ground meaning once and for all. But many philosophers and scholars, such as Ludwig Wittgenstein, W. V. O. Quine, John Dewey, Richard Rorty, and Thomas Kuhn, to mention only a few, have argued persuasively enough for me and many others that truth (capital T) and grounded meaning in any final or transcendental sense exceeds our grasp.[4]

I do not believe that all approaches to reading, interpretation, and criticism are equally valuable (this parallels the pragmatist rejection of the idea that all beliefs are equally valuable).[5] Raman Selden (1989) explained and demonstrated 24(!!!) approaches to literary theory and criticism. Which ones we choose—that is, which rhetorical strategies we employ—are to be determined, following the argument in Chapter 1, by our conceptions of satisfaction, fulfillment, and desire in the situations in which we find ourselves. I am not nor do I wish to be neutral when it comes to reading research. Feminist, critical, and deconstructive approaches were selected, in part, because each has much to offer contemporary educators. The approaches to reading that I favor lean toward those that are historical (missing here); interpretive analytic and genealogical after Foucault (also missing); deconstructive; and critical toward the end of promoting human dignity and community, which are always being reconstituted (see Cherryholmes, 1988, Chapter 8). No claim is made that the following three readings reveal any "essential" meaning of this research. Nor do these readings singly or jointly provide a "correct" reading of the research. The paradoxes, ambiguities, and contradictions that readers encounter in their attempts to clarify meanings require them to make choices. Where rational, these choices are pragmatic.[6]

Each of the three readings that follow attempt to provide an acceptable and persuasive reading-interpretation-criticism in terms of one strand each of feminist, critical, and deconstructive thought. Despite the fact that the following readings have been generated by a white male, I remind the reader that I reject the notion that there is a correct or essential feminist or critical or deconstructive reading. I do not believe, for example, that a "real" feminist could produce a nonproblematic reading that would capture the essence of feminist thought. My task is to explore the complexities involved in clarifying what research findings mean as premises for belief and action. Scholes (1989) wrote:

> To read at all, we must read the book of ourselves in the texts in front of us, and we must bring the text home, into our thought and lives, into our judgments and deeds. We cannot enter the texts we read, but they can enter us. . . . Such reading involves looking closely at the text (so closely, perhaps, as to alarm its protectors); it also involves situating the text, learning about it, seeing it among others of its kind; and first and last, reading requires us to make the text our own in thought, word, and deed. (p. 6)

We lost our way in reading research, I submit, when we became consumed with modernist illusions of a foundational epistemology and the promise of obtaining certain and objective knowledge. Paying attention to how we read, perhaps, can change the text of our research and our conversations about it. All texts, pragmatists emphasize, can be read differently, including the one you are reading.[7] How might different readers bring home the text of Palincsar and Brown (1984)?

Reciprocal Teaching

Annemarie Palincsar's and Ann Brown's (1984) study, "Reciprocal Teaching of Comprehension-Fostering and Comprehension-Monitoring Activities," stimulated considerable research on reciprocal teaching.[8]

> The basic procedure was that an adult teacher, working individually with a seventh-grade poor reader, assigned a segment of the passage to be read and either indicated that it was her turn to be the teacher or assigned the student to teach that segment. The adult teacher and the student then read the assigned segment silently. After reading the text, the teacher (student or adult) for that segment asked a question that a teacher or test might ask on the segment, summarized the content, discussed and clarified any difficulties, and finally made a prediction about future content. All of these activities were embedded in as natural a dialogue as possible, with the teacher and student giving feedback to each other. (pp. 124–125)

The way summarizing was depicted provides important insights into how they conceptualized reading and text. In the following quotations they explain how summarizing was taught and assessed and how they evaluated a student's ability to summarize:

> The adult teacher provided the guidance necessary for the student teacher to complete the preceding activities through a variety of techniques: *prompting*, "What question did you think a teacher might ask?"; *instruction*, "Remember, a summary is a shortened version, it doesn"t include detail"; and *modifying the activity*, "If you"re having a hard time thinking of a question, why don"t you summarize first?" (p. 131)

This is how they describe their assessment of summarizing. They were interested in measuring how students brought order to a text by identifying what was central or marginal in it:

> The students were . . . asked to indicate where any of five main condensing rules could be applied. The five rules were: (1) *deletion* of trivia; (2) *deletion* of redundancy; (3) *superordination*, where a list of exemplars was replaced with a superordinate term; (4) *selection* of a topic sentence to serve as a scaffolding of the summary, and (5) *invention* of a topic sentence for a paragraph where one was not explicitly stated. (pp. 133–134)

They concluded:

> It would appear that the continual instruction during training to *paraphrase prose segments by concentrating on the main idea* did lead to a significant transfer to a quite dissimilar task. (p. 150; emphasis added)

They repeatedly emphasized the elimination of trivia and redundancy, superordination, and "paraphrasing . . . by concentrating on the main idea." They brought to their study a specific view of reading and text.

Two studies were conducted. In the first study six students were assigned to a reciprocal teaching treatment group; six, to an untreated control group. At a later time six students were assigned to an alternative intervention group that focused on locating information; six, to a control group that involved practice with daily assignments. In the second study two classroom teachers and two resource room teachers were given three sessions of training in reciprocal teaching and, with the exception of variation in baseline instructions, four groups of students were given the same treatment. Major findings included: (1) "improvement in the students' dialogues"; (2) "improvement on the comprehension tests [that] was large and reliable"; (3) "the effect was durable"; (4) "the effect generalized to the classroom setting"; (5) there was "reliable transfer to laboratory tasks that differed in surface features from the training and assessment tasks"; (6) "sizable improvements in standardized comprehension scores were recorded"; (7) "intervention was . . . [also] successful in natural group settings conducted by regular teachers"; and (8) "teachers were uniformly enthusiastic about the procedure once they had mastered it" (pp. 167–168). This research article tells an impressive story. An intervention designed to improve reading comprehension—influenced, in part, by Vygotsky's work—was successfully implemented with seventh-grade students who had been poor readers. Impressive gains were measured on a variety of outcome measures. During a decade of reports of repeated failures in U.S. education, reciprocal teaching promised future successes.

In order to keep the following readings of manageable length, only the dependent variable is given detailed attention. In the language of research design, I focus on the construct validity, if you will, of the outcome measures or dependent variables, that in this case, are comprehension skills. An extended quotation reviews this aspect of the research:

> In a review of both the traditional reading education literature and recent theoretical treatments of the problem, we found that six functions were common to all . . . : (1) understanding the purposes of reading, both explicit and implicit; (2) activating relevant background knowledge; (3) allocating attention so that concentration can be focused on the major content at the expense of trivia; (4) critical evaluation of content for internal consistency, and compatibility with prior knowledge and common sense; (5) monitoring ongoing activities to see if comprehension is occurring, by engaging in such activities as periodic review and self-interrogation; and (6) drawing and testing inferences of many kinds, including interpretations, predictions, and conclusions. For the purpose of instruction, we selected four concrete activities that could

be engaged in by novice learners and that would embody the overlapping functions contained in points 1 through 6 above. These were *summarizing* (self-review), *questioning, clarifying,* and *predicting.* . . . In summary, these four activities were selected because they provide a dual function, that of enhancing comprehension and at the same time affording an opportunity for the student to check whether it is occurring. (pp. 120–121, emphasis in original)

Reciprocal teaching attempts to produce the orderly consumption of well-organized texts. The four activities of summarizing, questioning, clarifying, and predicting were conceptualized in terms of more or less well-formulated rules and procedures for bringing them about and for assessing them.

The pragmatist question, simply put, is: What do these findings mean? The assumption is that their findings as stated are true; that is, they are the most reasonable things to believe under the circumstances. They mean, I will argue, different things. Things that are not easily reconciled.

CHAPTER 8

One Feminist Reading of "Reciprocal Teaching"

Feminist theory and criticism (the theme of this chapter) and critical theory and deconstruction (the themes of the following two chapters) can each generate multiple readings of the same text.[1] What follows is one cultural or ecological feminist reading of Palincsar and Brown's research on reciprocal teaching.

Reciprocal teaching was designed for students who have difficulty reading. Feelings of concern and care for students who read poorly is embedded in reciprocal teaching. The rural—or, at least, nonurban—Illinois schools chosen for these studies reflect this. Furthermore, some of the anecdotal reports indicate how pleased teachers were as their slow-reading students learned to summarize, clarify, and delete trivia. Beneath the technical language of quasi-experimental research is a subtext of helping; this was not just a technical exercise in instruction or research. Furthermore, nonsexist language was used throughout. Pronouns were almost always female. But it is difficult to situate the research beyond these comments because the authors themselves did not do so. They chose the distanced voice of social scientific research.

Feminist concerns, however, extend well beyond avoiding sexist language. Carmen Luke (1992) has described the task that many feminist educational theorists set for themselves: They "have tended largely to focus on critiques of patriarchal assumptions and practices in efforts to document the politics and institutionalization of gendered differences in educational settings and discourses" (p. 25). Patriarchy, a system of thought and social organization, is arranged and ordered by recognizing the supremacy of the father or male. It can exhibit itself textually in a variety of ways. One way is to decontextualize what is written. Decontextualization is particularly male, the argument goes, and is related to the mutual reinforcement of a number of historical lineages: science, capitalism, and the rise of professionalism. Western thought has been dominated by men, white men. Both premodern and modern (before and after the beginning of the Enlightenment) discourses and practices have been patriarchal. The power and insight of modern thought derive, to a substantial degree, from its basis in formal rationality and science, and these discourses are patriarchal. Attempting to remove a text from its private context by appealing to the authority of formal rationality privileges male visions because generally it is men who are in positions of authority.

Decontextualizing a text invites patriarchal dominance by denying the connectedness of "women's ways of knowing" (see Belenky, Clinchy, Goldberger, & Tarule, 1986). Sandra Harding (1987) makes this argument:

> The best feminist analysis . . . insists that the inquirer her/himself be placed on the same critical plane as the overt subject matter. . . . That is, the class, race, culture, and gender assumptions, beliefs, and behaviors of the researcher her/himself must be placed within the frame of the picture that she/he attempts to paint. . . . We need to avoid the "objectivist" stance that attempts to make the researcher's cultural beliefs and practices invisible while simultaneously skewering the research objects, beliefs, and practices on the display board. (p. 9)

We have some general information about the cultural beliefs of Palincsar and Brown through their commitment to a particular type of research set in rural Illinois, but it was not situated in terms of class, gender, or ethnicity.

At the outset reciprocal teaching attended to private context by focusing on relevant background knowledge. It ended with relatively decontextualized public outcome measures. Reciprocal teaching begins, they wrote, "by discussing relevant background knowledge at the start of each instructional period" and proceeds by "embedding the instruction in the context of reading for the clear purpose of answering questions on the text" (Palincsar & Brown, 1984, p. 120). The goal of reciprocal teaching was to find the gist, the summary, the voice, the story in the text. They elaborated: "Thus, closing one's eyes (metaphorically) and attempting to state the gist of what one has read, and asking questions of *clarification, interpretation, and prediction* are activities that both improve comprehension and permit students to monitor their own understanding" (p. 121, emphasis added). Their first two condensing rules for writing summaries—(1) "deletion of trivia" and (2) "deletion of redundancy"—contributed to the push for decontextualized and public readings. On the other hand, detail, even if minor or repetitive, contributes to context and ambiance. It enhances possibilities for connection. The instruments were designed, it seems, to detect whether the students not only could read but also could produce an "essentialist" reading.

Outcome measures of success were decontextual and public. Students monitored themselves in pursuit of external goals. But the four activities of self-directed summarizing, questioning, clarifying, and predicting do not "require us to make the text our own in thought, word, and deed" because these activities are undertaken "for the clear purpose of answering questions on the text," for summarizing the "gist of what one has read." Univocal criteria that determine whether a summary is correct or incorrect are public. What is private are meanings generated when the text is made one's own. Susan Bordo (1987) gives one account of the modern origins of this distinction in her analysis of Descartes' *Meditations*:

> A new theory of knowledge, thus, is born, one which regards all sense experience as illusory and insists that the object can only truly be known by the perceiver who is willing to purge the mind of all obscurity, all irrelevancy, all free imaginative associations, and all passionate attachments. (p. 260)

Concluding her argument in a way at odds with teaching for "answering questions on the text," Bordo continued:

> Recent scholarly emergence and revaluation of epistemological and ethical perspectives that have been identified as feminine in classical as well as contemporary writing . . . claim a natural foundation for knowledge, not in detachment and distance, but in closeness, connectedness, and empathy. They find the failure of connection (rather than a blurring of boundaries) as the principle cause of breakdown in understanding. (p. 263)

The presumption that texts are univocal opens the door for distance, detachment, and the belief that all valuable knowledge is public.

Texts that deny gender present themselves as generic. They pretend to speak the truth, and truth is gender-neutral. Authoritative texts are distanced, objective, and have a single voice (otherwise they would not be authoritative); they are value-neutral, dispassionate, and controlling. *Androcentric* is a term sometimes applied to such texts. It comes from the combination of *andro* and *centric*, where *andro* refers to "man" or "male" and *centric* means "centered." Androcentric texts are sometimes called phallologocentric (Eagleton, 1983).

In describing her efforts to avoid a generic and patriarchal voice for teachers and students in the classroom, Elizabeth Ellsworth (1989) argued against the push for common, consensual, correct textual interpretations:

> What would it mean to recognize not only that a multiplicity of knowledges are present in the classroom as a result of the way difference has been used to structure social relations inside and outside the classroom, but that these knowledges are contradictory, partial, and irreducible? They cannot be made to "make sense"—they cannot be known, in terms of the single master discourse of an educational project's curriculum or theoretical framework. (p. 321)

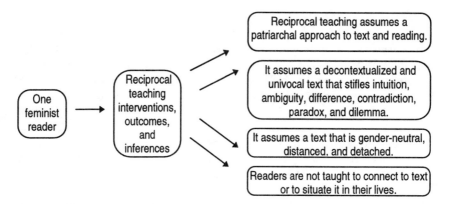

FIGURE 8.1. One feminist reader tracing in her imagination the conceivable practical consequences of reciprocal teaching.

A feminist educator might use reciprocal teaching strategies in order to understand a text on its own grounds, without agreeing with an author at the start or finish, although the idea of understanding a text is not itself well understood (see Gloversmith, 1984). And feminists might revise or supplement reciprocal teaching. But reciprocal teaching would not be driven by the educational product and outcome of answering questions about the text. The steps of summarizing, clarifying, questioning, and predicting, if not dropped altogether, could be augmented perhaps. Students and teachers could interpret the text in terms of their experiences. Because one of the readings dealt with snakes (reported in the article), students and teachers could describe, for example, experiences each has had with snakes. Attempts could be made to situate the text and its reading in the immediate setting of the classroom. The stories and the ways in which they are read can be made less detached and distanced. Teachers and students could also discuss and explore differences between reading for information and reading for pleasure, while noting that a hard-and-fast distinction between the two cannot be sustained—acquiring information is often pleasurable, and pleasurable experiences are often informative. A feminist educator might shift the emphasis from instruction to education, or the locus from "out there" to "in here," or to relational or interactional meanings that are constructed among readers, students, and teachers.

This reading of reciprocal teaching is diagrammed in Figure 8.1. It can be read as a feminist reader (1) accepting at face value the Palincsar and Brown findings, that is, their findings are reasonable to believe under the circumstances, and (2) tracing out the conceivable practical consequences of the Palincsar and Brown research from the feminist standpoint outlined above.

From this perspective of feminist theory and criticism, the pragmatist meaning of reciprocal teaching is that it constitutes patriarchal instruction (not the same as education). It teaches students to search for one voice in the text. It values public over private meanings. The desire for agreement on textual meanings stifles intuition, ambiguity, difference, contradiction, paradox, and dilemma to silence much that is called feminine. The slippery problem of construct validity, assigning words to measurements, functions in this instance to exclude feminine voices. Readers who score well on reciprocal teaching measurements learn to summarize, question, clarify, and predict *the* story in the text, while feminist theorists and educators claim that *the* stories of the West have been written by men who have kept women at the textual margins or have only referenced them in footnotes.

CHAPTER 9

One Critical Reading of "Reciprocal Teaching"

Critical pedagogy has never been well defined or constituted by a tightly knit set of ideas and practices. Its references have included at one time or another different versions of Marxism put forth by Antonio Gramsci and Louis Althusser; the critical theory of the Frankfurt School and the work of Jurgen Habermas; phenomenology and ethnography; critical ethnography; various approaches to literary criticism and theory; postmodernism; poststructuralism, including the work of Michel Foucault and Jacques Derrida; and feminist criticism. Many differences exist within as well as between these schools of thought. In this investigation I treat feminist and deconstructionist thought (one form of poststructuralism) separately from themes developed in the critical theory of the Frankfurt School, that, for present purposes, I call critical pedagogy. The themes and questions that shape this section are shared by many thinkers and will not, with few exceptions, be attributed to specific writers.

Critical theorists of the Frankfurt School emphasize that knowledge is not independent of human interests, work, and interaction. Critical educators attempt to disclose the underlying arrangements of social and political power and their justifying ideologies when it comes to what knowledge students learn. Attempts are then made to trace how power and ideologies of power weave through the hegemonic values and practices of education. Because critical theory developed in a Marxist tradition, many of its analyses have focused on the effects of social class on schooling. A well-known and widely cited example is Jean Anyon's (1980) study of the effects of social class in five elementary schools. Sometimes critical educators focus on a crisis interpretation of contemporary society and schooling. *OED* definitions of critical include, "Of the nature of, or constituting, a crisis: a. Of decisive importance to the issue. *spec. critical path*: the most important sequence of stages in an operation, [emphasis in original]" "Involving suspense or grave fear as to the issue: attended with uncertainty or risk," and "Tending to determine or decide: decisive, crucial." Also critical educators attend to criticism that the *OED* defines as, "The act of criticizing, or passing judgement upon the qualities or merits of anything" and "The art of estimating the qualities and character of literary or artistic work."

To begin, the Palincsar and Brown study is to be praised because it reports a successful method of teaching reading aimed at poor readers, and reading achievement scores are positively correlated with social class. Furthermore, reciprocal teaching encourages, teaches, and allows students to speak by way of role reversal. Students assume the role of teacher. But, as the feminist reading pointed out, reciprocal teaching teaches students to seek *the* meaning of a text. Reciprocal teaching does not teach interpretation or criticism. Its limited, if laudable, goals do not include "judicious evaluation" or "variant readings." Because reciprocal teaching portrays a text with only one message, it fails to help students "see a thing clearly and truly in order to judge it fairly." Palincsar and Brown might respond that their relatively simple and uncomplicated texts were basically informative and contained only one message. Only for purposes of argument will this point be granted. If it is the case that students transfer summarizing and questioning skills to other texts, as Palincsar and Brown conclude, and if students learn that texts have only one meaning, then when they encounter a literary or political or social text they will look for one meaning. Critical educators might argue that this is an example of the hidden curriculum, where poor readers are taught the use of a restricted linguistic code in the name of increased reading comprehension. Basil Bernstein (1979) wrote:

> Restricted codes are more tied to a local social structure and have a reduced potential for change in principles. Where codes are elaborated, the socialised has more access to the grounds of his own socialisation, and so can enter into a reflexive relationship to the social order he has taken over. Where codes are restricted, the socialised has less access to the grounds of his socialisation, and thus reflexiveness may be limited in range. *One of the effects of the class system is to limit access to elaborated codes.* (p. 478, emphasis in original)

Even if differences between restricted and elaborated codes are neither as well defined nor as class specific as Bernstein suggested, reciprocal teaching improves the reading skills of poor readers but does not develop their ability to use elaborated codes.

One critical interpretation of the effects of reciprocal teaching goes something like this: Teachers desire to do the best job they can and help students learn. Reciprocal teaching is effective in enhancing the reading comprehension of poor readers. Reciprocal teaching is used, it is effective, and students learn to look for a single story in the text. They do not learn interpretive or critical skills. Because textbooks and other authoritative texts are products of dominant classes and groups, students learn hegemonic accounts of social relations. If reciprocal teaching is successful, students will eventually act on the basis of dominant interpretations and explanations. This is generic social reproduction. Society reproduces itself along with its existing inequities and oppression because everyone acts rationally in their own best interest. It is arguable that reciprocal teaching is a dramatic instance in which a classically liberal policy that is designed to help individuals act within their social location ends up by reproducing privilege and inequality. Another effect of treating texts as univocal is to reify them. If texts are regarded as material and concrete, as naturally occurring instead of socially constructed, then texts have power over readers. When texts are reified, the job of the reader is to learn and adjust to the "natural" social order they present.

It is fashionable nowadays to speak of teacher and student empowerment. Some might claim that reciprocal teaching empowers students. For purposes of present discussion, power relationships are social, political, and material asymmetries or inequalities that induce actions by providing rewards or negative sanctions. If the relationship between a text and a reader is considered in terms of power, it is possible for the text to have power over the reader where students are rewarded or sanctioned depending upon whether they answer questions on the text. Reciprocal teaching promotes the power of the text over the reader. Granted, it is often useful to accede power to texts because texts in turn enhance the reader's power in other situations, from how to drive a car to how to cook an omelet to how to pour concrete. But there is an obvious downside. Feelings of alienation and boredom can result if students are continually asked to adapt to authoritative texts that often express cultural, ethnic, and class values different from those of the student.

Students acquire textual power when their interpretative and critical abilities tilt the asymmetries and inequalities between themselves and the text in their favor. Feminist and critical educators share many assumptions about the role of textual complexity in supporting current arrangements of social and political privilege and oppression. But one distinction that separates them, although many feminist educators think of themselves as critical educators and vice versa, is that each has a different agenda for reading the authority, power, themes, symbols, and literary tropes in the text. The agenda of one deals with gender, the other with class. And some feminist educators (Ellsworth, 1989; Luke, 1992) point out that male critical educators wish to tell them how to read. Patriarchy is alive and well, they say, among critical educators.

This reading of reciprocal teaching is diagramed in Figure 9.1. It can be read as a critical reader (1) accepting at face value the Palincsar and

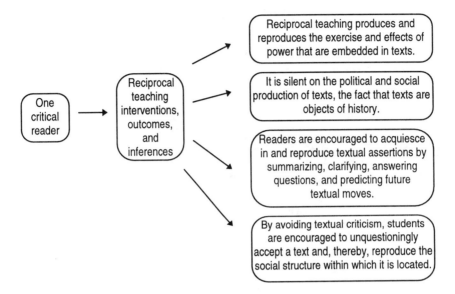

FIGURE 9.1. One critical reader tracing in her imagination the conceivable practical consequences of reciprocal teaching.

Brown findings, that is, the research findings are reasonable to believe under the circumstances, and (2) tracing out the conceivable practical consequences of the Palincsar and Brown research from the perspective of a critical educator or critical pedagogue. A critical educator who traces the consequences of reciprocal teaching may well assess them very differently from a feminist. The critic requires distance; the feminist, affiliation and connection. *Some critical educators will try to increase distance and detachment in order to understand and criticize oppressive social structures that texts present as "natural."* There is little doubt that various approaches to curriculum and education, such as critical-feminist or poststructural-feminist pedagogy, can be constructed. Major concerns of different readers, however, often push in different directions, producing a plurality of pragmatist readings and meanings.

A critical educator might revise reciprocal teaching by adding interpretation and criticism to the list of clarifying, summarizing, questioning, and predicting. A critical educator might attempt to de-reify texts by pointing to their social construction, observing that texts are products of history and power. Texts are never neutral to our interests. They draw our attention to some things and away from others. Those who write and authorize texts do so for a purpose. A critical educator might push in the direction of viewing texts as symbols of power and would encourage students to look for power in and behind a text. This requires students to ask: Who is speaking? Who listens? What is written? What is avoided? Which ideas are proposed as foundational? What is rewarded? What is penalized? Feminist and poststructural educators can also push questions such as these, although toward different ends.

Critical educators want students to be critics so that they can help emancipate themselves and others from oppressive social conditions. But reciprocal teaching does not promote criticism. It champions textual acquiescence. It is consistent with what Allan Bloom advocated in *The Closing of the American Mind*. Scholes (1989) put it like this:

> The great books of past ages, in the eyes of Bennett, Hirsch, and Allan Bloom, are to be mythologized, turned into frozen monuments of Greatness in which our "cultural heritage" is embodied. This is precisely what Bloom does to Plato, for instance, turning the dialectical search for truth into a fixed recipe for "greatness of soul." The irony of this is that Plato can only die in this process. (p. 125)

Read the text closely. Learn what it says. Do not question it. Critical educators, however, find advantage where reciprocal teaching begins. After students learn to summarize one story in a text, they can be taught that texts can be read and interpreted in order to detect the operations and effects of ideology, power, inequality, oppression, and injustice. Students can become critics and interpreters. They can seize textual power. The textual theory of reciprocal teaching camouflages textual disempowerment as reading comprehension.

CHAPTER 10

One Deconstructive Reading of "Reciprocal Teaching"

Deconstruction is the term for textual analysis that derives from a particular logical—or nonlogical, as it may more properly be called—property of language. The term *deconstruction* was first associated prominently with the work of the French philosopher Jacques Derrida. The reading of reciprocal teaching that follows is formulated, broadly speaking, in that tradition. It is important to note, however, that a powerful argument that parallels important deconstructive insights was made in modern logic and analytic philosophy at mid-century by the American philosopher and pragmatist W. V. O. Quine (1953/1971; I return to Quine's argument in Chapter 13). Exercising a fair amount of rhetorical simplification for the sake of brevity, one of Quine's key points was that the meaning of a word is always somewhat up in the air because we lack a clear characterization of natural-language analytic meanings (analyticity) and synonyms (synonymy). We know a word's synonym, Quine argued, by its usage. Usages change. This captures the temporal aspect of meaning that Derrida calls deferral of meaning.

There was a second aspect to Quine's argument. If we cannot give an analytic account of meaning, then we cannot give a formal account of translation. Complete and accurate translations preserve the meaning when one word or phrase is substituted for another. Quine pointed out that this is what we do not know how to do. Research requires translations whereby a theoretical term, say, "reading comprehension," is substituted for an observational term, say, "observed reading comprehension." Sometimes research findings report an indefinitely large number of substitutions, "*A* means *B* means *C* means *D* means . . . *N*." The effect, following Quine, is that we do not know whether whatever *A* means is fully captured by *B* or any subsequent translation. This is what Derrida calls dispersion of meaning. Together, deferral and dispersion constitute what Derrida calls *difference*. Texts are, it seems, out of the author's control. Language does not appear to be up to what we might wish to ask of it.

Authors rhetorically make claims for their texts, in the present case about improving reading comprehension. Because of the play of *difference*, the text by its own logic may controvert and contradict its rhetorical claims. *Differance* and the deconstructive moves it makes possible have a logical status not unlike $2 + 2 = 4$, although the point of *differance* is the lack of identity and presence instead of identity as found in an equation. Deconstruction, by itself, is nonprogrammatic. It is not possible to oppose it, as one might oppose Marxism or the Republican party platform or the pro-life movement. It is not possible to oppose deconstruction as a new orthodoxy because there is no deconstructive project to be orthodox about. It is a way of reading. It is reading for subtexts, for textual contradictions, for textual blockages, for that which was textually suppressed, and for that which was textually excluded. The issue is not whether to reject or not reject deconstruction, as one might a null hypothesis. The issue is what to do with it.

Terry Eagleton (1983) writes that

> Deconstruction . . . has grasped the point that the oppositions with which classical structuralism tends to work represent a way of seeing typical of ideologies. Ideologies like to draw rigid boundaries between what is acceptable and what is not, between self and non-self, truth and falsity, sense and nonsense, reason and madness, central and marginal, surface and depth. . . . Deconstruction tries to show how such oppositions, in order to hold themselves in place, are sometimes betrayed into inverting or collapsing themselves. . . . The tactic of deconstructive criticism . . . is to show how texts come to embarrass their own ruling systems of logic . . . by fastening on the "symptomatic" points, the *aporia* or impasses of meaning, where texts get into trouble, come unstuck, offer to contradict themselves. (pp. 133–134)

Here is one short example, before turning to Palincsar and Brown, of how a text got into trouble, came unstuck and offered to contradict itself. In his widely used and highly respected *Foundations of Behavioral Research* (1973), Fred Kerlinger wrote that his book:

> is a treatise on scientific research; it is limited to what is generally accepted as the scientific approach. It does not discuss historical research, legal research, library research, cultural research, philosophical inquiry, and so on. It emphasizes, in short, understanding scientific research problem solution. (p. viii)

In asserting a structural scientific/nonscientific distinction, he introduced a problem that he did not recognize, address, or solve. Here is Kerlinger's problem: Research procedures, practices, and results must be interpreted (judgments must be made about validity, generalizability, and applicability, for example); yet the scientific status of interpretation remains unclear because interpretation involves, at one time or another, historical, linguistic, library, literary, and philosophical research. To draw the point out, all research occurs in historical context. Theoretical constructs, hypotheses to be tested, and theories are objects of history. Furthermore, theories of empirical phenomena, by conventional standards, are required to be internally consistent and not contradictory. Decisions about consistency and contradictoriness are made by appealing to logic. Logic is a branch of philosophy. Scientific inquiry depends upon what Kerlinger called nonscientific discourses; thus the scientific/nonscientific distinction deconstructs.

Now to a deconstructive reading of Palincsar and Brown's (1984) research. In brief, their article transgressed their criteria; their rhetoric exceeded their logic and evidence. They claimed in their title that reciprocal teaching is concerned with comprehension-fostering and comprehension-monitoring activities, but readers are never told what constitutes reading comprehension *or* incomprehension. This is what they wrote:

> In this paper, we concentrate on improving students' ability to learn from texts. It is generally agreed that given reasonable facility with decoding, reading comprehension is the product of three main factors: (1) considerate texts, (2) the compatibility of the reader's knowledge and text content, and (3) the active strategies the reader employs to enhance understanding and retention, and to circumvent comprehension failures. (p. 118)

The third point completes a circular argument: Readers comprehend when comprehension failures are avoided; and when comprehension failures are not avoided, readers do not comprehend. In the absence of an independent characterization of comprehension (nor, it should be added, do they tell us what constitutes understanding), how can comprehension failures be identified?

Palincsar and Brown (1984) measured student ability to detect textual incongruities in a way that superficially resembled one deconstructive strategy, but they employed it toward a different end:

> For six of the stories [of eight], one line was anomalous with the title; the remaining two stories made sense. Four of the stories, three containing anomalous lines, were presented on the pretest and the remainder on the posttest. ... The students were told to read each line and say "yes" if the line made sense in the story, or "no" if the line didn't make sense. (p. 134)

Their operative theory of text required congruence between story title and story lines, that is, titles should not mislead one about what to expect in the text. A correct response on this measure is one in which a reader identifies incongruities between a story line and story title, indicating, presumably, that the story line should be excised from the text. In their view, a faulty text has anomalous lines. If the question that they asked of their students—"read each line and say 'yes' if the line made sense in terms of the title, or 'no' if the line didn't make sense"—were put to a reader of "Reciprocal Teaching of Comprehension-Fostering and Comprehension-Monitoring Activities," where the line of text was the title of the article itself, a comprehending reader, in terms of Palincsar and Brown's own research, would answer *"no." Is this inability to identify story-line anomalies to be attributed to the text of Palincsar and Brown or to the reader?*

Despite their failure to characterize reading comprehension, it was incumbent upon Palincsar and Brown to measure something they called reading comprehension. Here is their translation of the theoretical construct "reading comprehension" into "reading comprehension observed":

> In this series of studies, we decided to train the four activities of self-directed summarizing (review), questioning, clarifying, and predicting, embedding them in the context of a dialogue between student and teacher that took place during the actual task of reading with the clear goal of deriving meaning from the text. Each "separate" activity was used in response to a concrete problem of text comprehension. (p. 121)

Comprehension, in this account, occured when students engaged successfully in self-directed summarizing (review), questioning, clarifying, and predicting that were directed toward the goal of understanding and remembering the text content. Because no independent measure of understanding was used, comprehension reduced to remembering the text content was measured by successful summarizing, questioning, clarifying, and predicting. It is likely that a main idea question a teacher or a test might ask about Palincsar and Brown's research article would be: What is reading comprehension?

Palincsar and Brown described reciprocal teaching as a way for students with poor reading comprehension to start on the path to becoming mature readers:

> Mature readers can come to grips with a variety of inconsiderate texts, that is, those that creatively violate accepted structure or those that are just plainly poorly written. Mature readers also read to learn, that is, they read to obtain content knowledge that they do not yet possess. . . . Mature learners question and elaborate their own knowledge and the content of the text, testing their degree of understanding by thinking of counter-examples and testing possible generalizations, by attempting to apply their new found knowledge, and by a variety of debugging ploys that force them to correct their misunderstandings. . . . As there is ample evidence that such activities prove particularly

troublesome for the young and academically weak, attempts to instruct these activities seem particularly worthwhile. (pp. 119–120)

The reason they focused on "comprehension-fostering strategies is that they comprise a set of knowledge-extending activities that apply in a wide range of situations other than reading; these are the basic skills of argument" (p. 119). As described, however, reciprocal teaching does not teach readers to "come to grips with a variety of inconsiderate texts." For present purposes only will it be granted that their description of mature reading skills constitutes "the basic skills of argument," but reciprocal teaching does not teach these skills. Under the rhetoric of teaching reading comprehension, reciprocal teaching promotes technical and procedural reading skills such as summarizing and predicting.

Comprehension, at the outset the dominant term in their structural distinction of reading comprehension/technical reading skills, is addressed in terms of reading skills and processes and operations, such as providing a synopsis or questioning. Simultaneously, comprehension is distinct from—yet is measured by—reading skills. Reading comprehension is marginalized during the course of their research article, while purported instrumental operations at the textual margin—reading skills— are moved to a position of dominance. The argument and evidence reverse

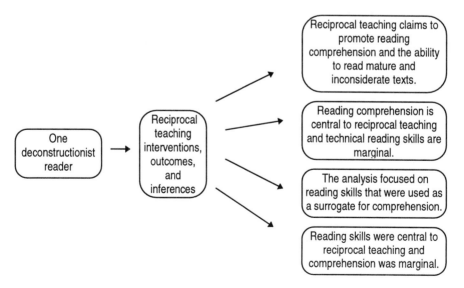

FIGURE 10.1. One deconstructionist reader tracing the conceivable practical consequences of reciprocal teaching.

the initial structural distinction, where reading comprehension was valued over technical reading skills, and replaced it with technical reading skills that are valued over reading comprehension.

   This reading of reciprocal teaching is diagramed in Figure 10.1. The diagram can be read as outlining some of the consequences of the Palincsar and Brown text that a reader who looks closely for textual blockages and inversions might point out. Whereas the feminist and critical readings accept the findings to determine the consequences for future practice, the deconstructionist reading looks closely at the text of the research for insight into what the text says about itself. What are the consequences of the Palincsar and Brown text for what the text claims? This question precedes those about the consequences of reciprocal teaching research for classroom practice.

   The logic of Palincsar and Brown invokes a diminished view of text. If reciprocal teaching reading skills transfer, say, to the humanities and social studies, then the textual complexity and opportunities for interpretation and criticism—from a Shakespeare play to a presidential address—will be missed. Palincsar and Brown rhetorically promise much more in the name of comprehension-fostering and comprehension-monitoring activities than they deliver. Their title suggests that reciprocal teaching helps students to gain power over a text when just the opposite seems to be the case. Reciprocal teaching fosters textual acquiescence. The conceivable practical consequences of reciprocal teaching contradict its proclaimed goals.

CHAPTER 11

Truth, Meanings, Rhetoric, and Pragmatism

The Palincsar and Brown research and the preceding feminist, critical, and deconstructive readings are, in my reading, all pragmatist exercises. Each clarified the meaning of a text by tracing its conceivable practical consequences.[1] The researchers and the various interpretations each contained conceptions of beauty. They alternately pushed in the direction of decoding words, connecting with the text, criticizing socially oppressive relations, and opposing textual fundamentalism. Different and contradictory meanings were produced because different readers had distinctive conceptions of satisfaction and fulfillment. In some sense, as noted above, we are all pragmatists. But pragmatism is rejected if orthodoxies—whether they are "scientific" or feminist or critical—become privileged, over tracing consequences. To favor dogma rather than tracing consequences assumes that we know the future and that it will be like the past.

Pragmatists believe that they and others must choose and act without knowing whether they or anyone else have got things "right." They have no idea what getting things "right" means, other than realizing expected outcomes. But assume the contrary for purposes of argument. Let us suppose that it is possible to get the facts straight—say, in the matter of reciprocal teaching—and that we have done so. The pragmatist task of clarifying what the facts mean, what their conceivable practical consequences are, remains. Knowing the facts (the facts can be generalized to include theories and explanations) and thereby solving the empiricist's problem exempts no one from deciding what they mean. Because pragmatists speak and act from specific and concrete standpoints, they never escape the problem of deciding what truths—which I interpret as what it is most reasonable to believe under the circumstances—mean.

Facts have consequences—some are realized, some imagined, and some beyond imagination. The pragmatist's job as artist and experimenter is to imagine satisfying, fulfilling, and beautiful consequences of facts in order to avoid unsatisfying, unfulfilling, and ugly outcomes. For example, some people who read the research on reciprocal teaching will interpret it as producing beautiful outcomes straightaway because of improved performance on reading tests. But the facts cannot tell us what to do. Another reader, say, a feminist, might interpret the research as stultifying in its truncated view of text and reading. It is the reader who anticipates the future. Facts provide opportunities as well as impose constraints on discourse about consequences.

Getting research findings and research methodology straight lets us know, more or less, which facts to take seriously and which facts are not, in fact, "facts." Robust research findings are valuable because they tell us which concepts, theories, models, narratives, and facts to take seriously. Sound research and what makes it so—issues that are endlessly debated (one fashionable debate is between quantitative and qualitative researchers)—save us from confusing fantasy observations from those that are more "objective." Once the facts are presented (recall that pragmatists are anti-essentialists; each event or object can be described in an indefinitely large number of ways where each in their turn has a set of supporting facts), pragmatists choose among rhetorical strategies that are feminist or critical or deconstructive or linguistically or statistically structural or historical or rational analytic or some combination of these or otherwise. Each offers insight. Each provides a lens. Reading to clarify meanings by pursuing consequences and forsaking essentialist, representationalist, and foundationalist conceits necessarily looks beyond provincial and parochial categories, interests, boundaries, and narratives.

Small-*t* truth and meaning are not distinct. Any proposed truth/ meaning or fact/meaning distinctions turn out to be charades. If we choose to treat meanings as truths, we do so for pragmatic purposes. What we decide to accept as truths, what is most reasonable to believe, are themselves meanings and meaningful. They result from observations and inferences. Research findings—whether they are empiricist, interpretive, critical, historical, philosophical, or some combination of these or others—are socially constructed. Even though research findings may circulate as truths, they are meanings in the pragmatist sense. They are themselves consequences of inquiry. Researchers make and record observations and then make decisions about their conceivable practical consequences. But researchers are not obligated to push the envelope, as it were, in exploring the consequences of their interventions and measurements and analyses. Thus, others are invited to look for additional stories in the texts of research.

Not only do meanings attach to research findings, but they are meanings that have been constructed, edited, and revised within the effects of power, institution, language, class, gender, and ethnicity, for example. What counts as true and what it means are different perhaps, if not distinct, because they look to different consequences. The first (truths) look to the consequences of what it is most reasonable to believe, and the second (pragmatist meanings) look to the conceivable practical consequences of what it is most reasonable to believe.

At this point the genealogical pragmatism of John Stuhr (1997) is pertinent. He frames his genealogical pragmatism as a pragmatist's response to postmodern challenges. The challenge, he writes, is "to make explicit the exclusions, oppositionalities, and the single-mindedness embedded in pragmatism's own notions of community, inquiry, and pluralism . . . to recognize the delimitations and violence of all ideals, and to remain open to multiple deconstructions of their own ideals even as they engage in the reconstruction of those ideals . . . [and] the formations of subjects, the discourses of rationalization, and the perspectival political differences at work in pragmatism's own will to intimacy" (p. 110). He calls genealogical pragmatism a disrobed pragmatism that produces (1) a history of the present (conceptions, desires, values, beliefs), (2) a genealogy of our problems, and (3) an analysis of exclusions in any problem-solution (p. 112). And, specifically to the point of meanings and truths, he observes that, "because truth is a collection of truths, a genuinely genealogical pragmatism must recognize that the philosopher-messenger who enlarges the meanings contained in provincial tongues is also a messenger who speak a provincial tongue—a different, but still provincial tongue" (p. 113). Each reading of Palincsar and Brown sought meaning in a provincial tongue, and each enlarged upon the meaning of the text. The article itself was written in a provincial tongue.

The preceding argument can be shortened:

1. Research; such as on reciprocal teaching and its constitutive theories and conceptions of reading, text, and teaching (modeling, role reversal) and learning and assessment (summarizing, clarifying, questioning, and predicting); if persuasive, produces truths (what is most reasonable to believe).
2. Statements that function as true (what is most reasonable to believe) are themselves produced by attempts to determine what something (a theory or concept or practice) means (what outcomes follow from affirming it).
3. Truths about practices, such as reciprocal teaching research, generate meanings that are the conceivable consequences (Peirce) of those truths.
4. The set of conceivable practical consequences of a theory, concept, or practice subsumes and exceeds the set of what is reasonable to believe about it.

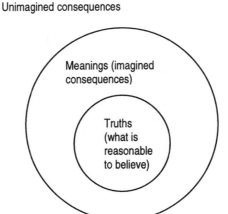

FIGURE 11.1.   Meanings and Truths.

5. Truths are pragmatically meaningful because they are conceivable consequences; but not all meanings (conceivable consequences) are reasonable to believe.

Meanings and truths constantly generate each other. *Pragmatists seek to expand their universe of meanings* (conceivable consequences) because they are interested in results. They may find that some conceptions that previously had been unimagined are useful and desirable, from quantum mechanics to feminist criticism. This leads pragmatists to be inclusive and democratic as argued in Chapter 6. *Pragmatists are driven to separate truths from fantasies* because they are interested in results. If one is interested in outcomes, it is important to decide which meanings are reasonable to believe and which are not. Because meanings and truths are constructed they are artistic creations and subject to aesthetic as well as scientific criticism—What meanings will we allow into our discourses? Which meanings will we systematically investigate?

AESTHETICS AND ETHICS

The relationship between what circulates as true and the aesthetics of alternative research methodologies was introduced in Chapter 5. A quick review observes that empiricist research methodologies are designed to enhance control, productivity, and efficiency (they often emphasize quantitative research skills). They produce facts that are likely to be embraced by those who are interested in control and productivity, say, by those who subscribe to certain schools of organizational and administrative thought and practice that value accountability and performance. Likewise, interpretive research methodologies generate facts about social understanding and communication (that many times result from qualitative investigations). These investigations are likely to be undertaken by those who believe that affiliation and connection are important, say, by ecological feminists who might subscribe to the first reading of reciprocal teaching. Critical research methodologies emphasize emancipation and enlightenment (that are promoted by critical researchers). These are likely to be favored, say, by those who valorize issues of social justice and equity. These few references to alternative research methodologies provide a second reason to reject truth/meaning and fact/meaning distinctions. Researchers decide which observations to collect and which facts warrant investigation. They choose what to research in substantial degree, I submit, on the basis of their aesthetic judgments (power contributes importantly to these values) about the consequences of generating one fact instead of a different one.

Another distinction that turns out to be illusory is that between ethical commitments—say, those of ecological feminists and critical researchers—and rhetorical strategies—say, those employed by deconstructive readers or empiricist, interpretive, or critical researchers. For present purposes I follow Scholes's (1989) textual characterization of ethics and rhetoric in terms of reading and writing. Ethics are "questions of the functions, effects, and ends of writing and reading. What is reading *for*?" (p. 90, emphasis in original). Rhetoric is "a textual economy, in which pleasure and power are exchanged between producers and consumers of texts, always remembering that writers must consume in order to produce and that readers must produce in order to consume" (p. 90).

Ethical commitments and rhetorical strategies are different, as are meanings and truths, but it is a mistake to believe that they are structurally distinct. Ethical commitments implicate rhetorical strategies and rhetorical strategies, ethical commitments. A feminist ethic, for example, will identify some rhetorical expressions, arguments, symbols, aspirations, and desires as more valuable than others. As a result, feminist readers may be drawn to rhetorics that are sensitive to subtexts, textual multivocality, ambiguity, connection, and contradiction and be less concerned with stability, convergence, hierarchy, and consensus. The reverse is also the case: Rhetorical strategies imply ethical positions. For example, interpretation is a rhetorical act, an act of textual economy and exchange, that requires readers to make choices. Choices cannot be made without reference to values and standards that, in turn, have ethical components.

Readings that employ the rhetorical strategies of deconstruction, for example, implicate some ethical stances and not others. Deconstructive rhetoric requires an ethic that is anti-essentialist and nonabsolute, that is continually expecting, if not experiencing, the construction and revision of meanings. Deconstructive readings reject ethical commitments that claim to be foundational and totalizing. The rhetoric of pragmatism also suggests a nonfundamentalist ethic of inclusiveness, mutual tolerance and respect, and meaningful communication that is reminiscent of but exceeds First Amendment values. Connections between pragmatism and democracy are both obvious and elusive, direct and diffuse, and "is marked . . . by exchanges of power and pleasure" (Scholes, 1989, p. 108).

Rorty (1991) gave the following warning to those who desire ideologically pure and univocal readings and meanings.

> Suppose that for the last three hundred years we had been using an explicit algorithm for determining how just a society was, and how good a physical theory was. Would we have developed either parliamentary democracy or relativity physics? Suppose that we had the sort of "weapons" against the fascists of which Dewey was said to deprive us—firm, unrevisable, moral principles which were not merely "ours" but "universal" and "objective." How could we avoid having these weapons turn in our hands and bash all the genial tolerance out of our own heads? (p. 43)

Pragmatically reading research or anything else requires tolerance and inclusiveness. Pragmatists are not extremists; neither do they countenance dictators. Pragmatists are democrats whom modern professions and research practices sometimes seek to police and subdue.

PRAGMATISM AND DECONSTRUCTION

If texts deconstruct, if anticipated consequences are texts, then pragmatist texts about consequences, truths, and meanings deconstruct. The pragmatist response is that not all texts deconstruct in all ways. It is possible that a deconstruction of research findings, policies, or protocols is simply not related to our aesthetic visions, goals, or purposes. Some deconstructions are likely to be so marginal to our purposes that they will hold no interest for us. A deconstructive reading can be an exciting rhetorical tour de force yet be of little interest to an individual reader. A deconstructive exercise may say more about the political and professional milieu of the research than about its practical consequences. Deconstructive readings are continually useful, however, because they remind us of the dangers of orthodoxy and the seductive appeal of hierarchy and authority.

It is an indication of how far removed, divorced, and alienated contemporary empiricists are from pragmatism that questions about "getting things right" dominate contemporary discourses on research and questions of meaning, aesthetics, ethics, power, and rhetoric are evaded. Aesthetic questions about whether research outcomes promote beautiful or ugly practices seem so odd that they appear to be almost completely out of place in conducting or reading research. Only an occasional reference to the elegance of a theory or explanation is found in the research literature, and these rare statements are almost always about the theory, not about the practices under investigation. Our research tradition sometimes gives the impression that questions of meaning are disposed of once questions of fact have been determined. And then there is power. Power produces and is reproduced by our practices, language, texts, and subjectivities. Power invades our readings, and we have yet to learn how to expel it and strongly suspect that it is impossible to do so. Power is found in the unequal relationships that constitute our social world. It circulates when we share interpretations, criticisms, and readings. Power is always already present when consequences and their aesthetics are imagined.

As pragmatists engage in discourses on the consequences of thinking, they continually face problems. They must decide whether the consequences they imagine are reliable or are mythical. They must choose among the wide range of aesthetic values that they can imagine. They must communicate their thoughts to others and negotiate their way through purported meanings and truths, ethics and rhetorics, standpoints, evidence, arguments, and alternative visions. There are no final answers.

In some ways, as previously noted, we have always been pragmatists—in our research and our reading. We have been choosing our community and a way of life in doing what we do. Among our conceits, however, have been claims to an epistemologically (say positivism or empiricism) or dogmatically superior (say an immanent socialism) position in order to deny, evade, and exclude the instabilities, uncertainties, terror, and responsibilities that accompany pragmatism. The emperor or empress, as you wish, of educational action and knowledge is not clothed with privileged knowledge, ethical certainties, grounded meanings, univocal conceptions of beauty, or with Truth, protestations to the contrary notwithstanding. The positions that have been called positivism and empiricism were always problematic. Increasingly it will be difficult to deflect the claim or escape the knowledge that we have been choosing our future as we have described and explained our past. We were unwitting pragmatists in our choices but not pragmatic at all in our arrogant and presumptive search for certainty as we tried to "get things right." We have been choosing a way of life and not simply generating knowledge with our research and how we read it. We are responsible for the stories we find within, upon, and against the texts of research. That has always been the case, but the luxury of self-delusion, if not intoxicating, has been a potent and often pleasant sedative. It was never possible to deny the obligations of reading, but our past is full of heroic efforts to read poorly. An inability to accept the obligations of reading has always resided within us.

PRAGMATISM/ANALYTIC PHILOSOPHY/PROGRAM EVALUATION

It is fair to ask if the renewed interest in pragmatism is simply another fad. I believe not. This time around pragmatism is likely to have a fair amount of staying power. It offers a way of being in the world that is neither ephemeral nor transient, even though it will likely be reinterpreted indefinitely. Part IV provides reasons for believing this. Pragmatism, I believe, is a natural outcome (consequence) of the modern era that began in the sixteenth and seventeenth centuries. Chapter 12 gives an account of modernity, from which pragmatism along with poststructuralism and postmodernity descend. Chapter 13 discusses important twentieth-century arguments made by W. V. O. Quine and Donald Davidson at the height of the modern era that presage a transition from analytic (modern, if you will) to postanalytic (postmodern) philosophy. They opened the way for a reexamination of pragmatism. Their arguments pointed to a reduced role of logic and an increased role of rhetoric in scientific arguments. Chapter 14 goes on to something entirely different, program evaluation in education. The results of hundreds of program evaluations document the decreased utility of discrete interventions and emphasize the importance of context and institutional development in educational change. The move from analytic to postanalytic philosophy (shifting from logic to rhetoric as well as deconstructing a purported distinction between them) and from specific interventions to institutional development (shifting attention from text to context suggesting a deconstruction of their proposed distinctiveness) reinforce the claim that pragmatism is not just another style that will soon disappear.

CHAPTER 12

Pragmatism and Its Ambiguous Link to Modernity

Richard Rorty, as quoted earlier, sees pragmatists and deconstructionists as natural allies, with neither having precedence over the other.[1] I agree and disagree. Pragmatists, poststructuralists, and postmodernists are natural allies indeed. But neither poststructural nor postmodern thought entails pragmatism as Peirce and Dewey described it and as I read it. They do not imagine practical consequences or experiment for the sake of beauty, for example. If one begins with pragmatism, however, its inductive, anti-essentialist, and fallibilist characteristics lead to and benefit from poststructural and postmodern insights and themes. Pragmatism is unthinkable without the poststructural and postmodern. The reverse is not the case.

Thinking about educational change itself is changing. It is undergoing a slow, sometimes painful, reconceptualization as it transitions from modern to pragmatist educational thought and practice.[2] It is a halting passage because much of the rhetoric of educational reform endorses and seeks to implement modernist assumptions and practices. A theme of many reform arguments is that our schools would be successful if we could make them fully modern (Labaree, 1997). I use the term *modern* as it might be used to describe a contemporary bureaucracy that is rational and hierarchical; that has clear lines of authority, fragmented tasks, and a body of expert knowledge and skills in the hands of administrators and staff; and where systematic reforms can be implemented and evaluated. Reform agendas often seek to make our schools more fully professional, accountable, rational, and on-task. My argument is that quite possibly we have glimpsed the limits of educational modernity. I do not contest the claim that many schools could benefit by becoming more modern and professional. But there are limits to what more accountability and standardization and rationality can bring. Pragmatism poses an alternative to structuralist and modernist reforms. But, first, what does it mean to be modern?

The word *modern* has derivatives that include *modernity, modernism,* and *modernization.* These words have been appropriated by many discourses and practices, including but extending well beyond education. The *OED* defines *modern* as

"Being at this time; now existing,"
"Of or pertaining to the present and recent times," and
"Of a movement in art and architecture, or the works produced by such
   a movement: characterized by a departure from or a repudiation of
   accepted or traditional styles and values."

In these usages *modern* means what is going on now, what is latest, and what is contemporary.

The term *modernity* is often used to refer to the rationalization of Western societies that began with the Enlightenment and the rise of modern science in the seventeenth and eighteenth centuries. Writing of Enlightenment intellectuals—including John Locke, Jean Jacques Rousseau, David Hume, and the Marquis de Condorcet, among many others—Isaiah Berlin (1990) gave the following description of some of the beliefs Enlightenment thinkers shared:

> They [Enlightenment thinkers] believed in varying measure that men were, by nature, rational and sociable; or at least understood their own and other's best interests when they were not being bamboozled by knaves or misled by fools; that, if only they were taught to see them, they would follow the rules of conduct discoverable by the use of ordinary human understanding; that there existed laws which govern nature, both animate and inanimate, and that these laws, whether empirically discoverable or not, were equally evident whether one looked within oneself or at the world outside. They believed that the discovery of such laws, and knowledge of them, if it were spread widely enough, would of itself tend to promote a stable harmony both between individuals and associations, and within the individual himself. . . . They believed that all good and desirable things were necessarily compatible, and some maintained more than this—that all true values were interconnected by a network of indestructible, logically interlocking relationships. The more empirically minded among them were sure that a science of human nature could be developed no less than a science of inanimate things, and that ethical and political questions, provided that they were genuine, could in principle be answered with no less certainty than those of mathematics and astronomy. A life founded upon these answers would be free, secure, happy, virtuous, and wise. (p. 60)

Much of the contemporary discourse about education and educational change arguably, many would say proudly, continues in this tradition that began some 300 to 400 years ago.

For a third approach to what it means to be modern, I draw on John McGowan's (1991) description of events associated with the Enlightenment:

> The challenge to Catholicism by the various Protestant sects, the challenge to Eurocentrism in the discovery of radically different societies in other parts of the globe, the challenge to religion manifested in both new scientific discoveries and new economic practices, the challenge to monarchy/oligarchy in the rise of popular, democratic agitation, and the challenge to traditional patterns of social integration in changing modes of production and distribution and the growth of towns and cities all combine over a three-hundred-year period (1500–1800) to transform Europe. By the end of this period, the West has recognized, in the face of diversity and change, that it is thrown back upon itself to ground, legitimate, and make significant its own practices. (p. 4)

McGowan later added:

> Modernity isolates the individual by encouraging the notion of autonomous, innate (or at least self-developed) qualities that then explain the individual's social accomplishments; the necessary corollary of this isolation is an institutional order that examines, differentiates among, and rewards these various selves. . . . Autonomy is socially created and socially rewarded in modernity. (pp. 248–249)

One consequence of the weakening of traditional religious and subject relationships during the Enlightenment and the rise of democracy and spread of capitalism was the rise of individuals who were increasingly independent and autonomous. Such independence and autonomy created a need to justify and legitimate one's activities and life because science, capitalism, and democracy prevented one from turning, in secure confidence, to the church, guild, or tribe for final and foundational meanings.

If the transition of Western social, political, and economic arrangements from traditional to modern brought advantages, it also generated new problems and ways of studying the world. Here is Raymond Apthorpe's (1985) take on modernization:

> Updating, upgrading, renovation, reconstruction or stabilization in the face of adverse social, physical or economic structures. . . . Often all that is meant is professionalism, rationality, planning or progress in general. (p. 532)

He continued:

> Modernization can often be best understood not as a particular development—or development theory or method for the study of development or development theory—but rather as a recurring pattern of perennial speech about such development, theory and method, and would-be practical action.

> In many development studies and policies this tends to be discourse about solutions which are more likely to be in search of, than for, problems. Whose discourse is this? On the whole this is the perennial speech *of* modernizing elites as well as *about* modernizing elites. (p. 532, emphasis in original)

This suggestion is remarkable: Modernization is a "recurring pattern of perennial speech" where the motivation to be rational, logical, scientific, and utility-maximizing in seeking progress, profits, accountability, and value-added outcomes produces behavior where solutions *precede* the search for problems, which they, our previously identified solutions, can answer. In Apthorpe's view of modernization, current elites—professional educators are one such elite—tend to propose answers to problems that they are allowed to frame. Because they were educated, trained, certified, and work in a modern profession, up-to-date educators necessarily think in largely modernist terms as they interact in modernist discourses and practices.

Vaclav Havel (1992) summarized important characteristics and subsequent problems of the modern world that developed from the Enlightenment in a speech he delivered to a United Nations secretariat:

> The modern era has been dominated by the culminating belief that the world . . . is a wholly knowable system governed by a finite number of universal laws that man can grasp and rationally direct for his own benefit. This era, beginning in the Renaissance and developing from the Enlightenment to socialism, from positivism to scientism, from the Industrial Revolution to the information revolution, was characterized by rapid advances in rational, cognitive thinking. This, in turn, gave rise to the proud belief that man, as the pinnacle of everything that exists, was capable of objectively describing, explaining and controlling everything that exists, and of possessing the one and only truth about the world. It was an era in which there was a cult of depersonalized objectivity, an era in which objective knowledge was amassed and technologically exploited, an era of belief in automatic progress brokered by the scientific method. It was an era of systems, institutions, mechanisms, and statistical averages. It was an era of ideologies, doctrines, interpretations of reality, an era in which the goal was to find a universal theory of the world, and thus a universal key to unlock its prosperity. . . . [However] We all know civilization is in danger. . . . We are looking for an objective way out of the crisis of objectivity. . . . [But] We cannot discover a law or theory whose technical application will eliminate all the disastrous consequences of the technical application of earlier laws and technologies. (p. 15)

Modern ways of looking at the world objectify it in a search for knowledge and control. They do what they set out to do. A characteristic of modern professions that is found in both Havel's and Apthorpe's views, then, is that modern professionals tend to look for and specify problems that objectified solutions can address, if not solve.

There are several ways in which modern inquiries in search of "an objective way out of the crisis of objectivity" play out in education. Sometimes the desire for a rational technology of educational change and innovation exhibits itself in attempts to be ultraorganized and systematic—such as stating goals, describing tasks designed to bring them about, breaking tasks into component parts, evaluating outcomes following task implementation, and introducing modifications based upon evaluations (Tyler, 1949). We live in an era of "systems," to use Havel's term, of change and innovation that seek to counteract the failed "systems" of the past. Contemporary efforts at educational change are a series of thoroughly modern adventures.

These adventures have met with qualified success, at best—a series of flawed modern quests, perhaps. Several explanations, to invoke a modern usage of this term, can be offered for the lack of success in modernizing our educational system and schools. Some failures can be attributed to the fact that many of these change efforts were not sufficiently modern. Some were due to the fact that various goals and objectives were not specified with sufficient clarity or precision to permit an adequate description and implementation of instrumental tasks. Some were due to the fact that insufficient resources were available to permit adequate planning and implementation. Some resulted from goals and objectives that were never adhered to with sufficient consistency, thereby blocking their systematic implementation and proper evaluation. Or it could be that many change proposals were not supported by teachers, principals, neighborhood groups, and others requisite for their success. Or perhaps the necessary expertise in terms of research findings and expert personnel was simply unavailable.

Modernist impulses have metamorphosed into something that some people now call postmodernism. The *OED* defines the prefix *post-* as "after, afterwards, subsequently" and "following, succeeding." Thus postmodernism refers, say, to something that has occurred after an up-to-date lifestyle or outlook. These definitions are useful in pointing our thinking in a given direction, more or less, but leave much unsaid. They suggest a crisis of representation, which pragmatists readily acknowledge (see Chapter 5), when traditional standards no longer apply. Epistemological and existential issues of knowledge and experience are defined not so much in themselves but by what they come after. Thus the meanings of *postmodern, poststructural, postindustrial, postcolonial*, and *postanalytic* are, in large part, responses to what was modern, structural, industrial, colonial, and analytic.

Examples of modern architecture, such as the skyscraper, provide one relatively clear example of what it means to be modern. Modern skyscrapers are functional. They do not indulge in wasted decoration or bow to traditions or conventions. Modernist thinking about architecture was hailed as a genuine discovery that exposed the "falseness" of previous architecture. Premodern views about architecture were false because they had been both less and more than purely functional. Postmodern skyscrapers—say, the earthquake-resistant pyramidal-shaped Trans-America Building in San Francisco that appears frequently in television advertisements—return to ornamentation and premodern conceptions. The pyramid that serves as the entrance to the Louvre in Paris is likewise a postmodern gesture. Postmodern buildings, in opposition to those that aspire to be modern, do not claim to be true. A postmodern architectural premise, one that is also definitely pragmatist, is that there is not just one way of building.

A related postmodern discovery, that parallels the role of the aesthetic in pragmatism, is that modernism is just another style. There are only styles. Postmodernism itself is a style. One pragmatist observation on this postmodern point about the proliferation of styles is that some styles are more beautiful or efficient or emotive or accountable or sensual than others. *Different styles have different consequences.* Living in a postmodern world does not excuse us from choosing among them. The choices, as argued previously, are artistic and experimental. Many styles (including pragmatist or postmodern) are available to educators. Educators, as well as architects, are artists. Their practice is their *objet d'art*.

Postmodern ideas have also influenced literary theory and criticism in ways that provide insight for educators. H. Aram Veeser's (1988) characterization of the new historicism contains several postmodern elements. According to Veeser, new historicism assumes:

1. that every expressive act is embedded in a network of material practices;

2. that every act of unmasking, critique, and opposition uses the tools it condemns and risks falling prey to the practice it exposes;

3. that literary and non-literary texts circulate inseparably;

4. that no discourse, imaginative or archival, gives access to unchanging truths nor expresses inalterable human nature;

5. finally . . . a critical method and a language adequate to describe culture under capitalism participate in the economy they describe. (p. xi)

Postmodern features of new historicism include the idea that we are unable to escape the effects of culture, history, and power, as Enlightenment thinkers desired and thought possible. Educators and architects, as well as literary theorists and critics, are products of as well as producers of culture, history, and power. Professional activities in education are cultural and historical, and they enact both the effects and exercise of power. Following this line of thinking, education has always been a postmodern as well as a modern enterprise; the postmodern elements simply went unnoticed or were interpreted as mistakes and errors. One result is that what was once familiar and taken for granted—education as a modernist project—becomes strange and mysterious. It awaits exploration and construction or vice versa.

What difference does any of this make for educators? For much of the twentieth century, efforts to describe, explain, and prescribe theories and practices of education have been couched in a modernist rhetoric that has highlighted rationality, hierarchy, expertise, accountability, and differentiation in order to promote progress and productivity. Understanding pragmatism, I believe, requires understanding how modernity has changed into postmodernity. Here is an outline of one version of this story, that I tell more fully in the following chapter: Modernism and rationality assume distinctions between logic and rhetoric, planning and spontaneity, text and context. Empiricism granted a central role to logic in validating theories, practices, and discourses. Rhetoric was relegated to the lesser tasks of persuasion and politics—say, implementation and staff development in education. We are required to abandon a logic/ rhetoric distinction, however, because of developments in modern logic. This comes as a result of trying to clarify what a logic/rhetoric distinction means. Asserting a logic/rhetoric distinction was a dogma and orthodoxy of empiricist research. It is seemingly gone. The effect for educators and others is that we are forced to think about the world in a way that relies less on logic to validate our conceptions and more on rhetoric to persuade ourselves and others about the world and how it operates. This is a move from a predominantly modern to a postmodern way of thinking. If educators make such a pragmatist and postmodern move—and I argue that they will, sooner or later—they will be required to criticize, reinterpret, and, possibly, reject at times conceptions of rationality, hierarchy, expertise, accountability, and differentiation that many, if not most, of them were trained to value and promote.

In broad terms, the modern/postmodern distinction and its subsequent deconstruction is associated with structural/poststructural, analytic/postanalytic, and colonial/postcolonial distinctions and deconstructions. What is known as postmodern or poststructural or postanalytic was always already present in what was called modern and structural and analytic. How were postmodern ideas always already contained in modern arguments, and how did they manage to remain hidden? I discuss these matters in the following chapter.

CHAPTER 13

Pragmatism and Its Unambiguous Link to Analytic Philosophy

Analytic philosophers have stated their intellectual problems with considerable clarity and rigor. They have pursued them diligently, sometimes with great brilliance. I review two classic articles, one by W. V. O. Quine and the second by his student Donald Davidson, that moved analytic philosophy in the direction of pragmatism and postanalytic philosophy. Their work is instructive for pragmatists and nonpragmatists alike.

Early in the twentieth century philosophy took a so-called linguistic turn. Richard Rorty (1967), in an introduction to an edited volume of illustrious essays entitled *The Linguistic Turn*, described the work in the following passage:

> [By] the . . . recent philosophical revolution, that of linguistic philosophy, I shall mean . . . the view that philosophical problems are problems which can be solved (or dissolved) either by reforming language, or by understanding more about the language we presently use. This view is considered by many of its proponents to be the most important philosophical discovery of our time, and, indeed, of the ages. By its opponents, it is interpreted as a sign of the sickness of our souls, a revolt against reason itself, and a self-deceptive attempt (in Russell's phrase) to procure by theft what one has failed to gain by honest toil. (p. 3)

Some educators might be tempted to say as much about those among us, including myself, who are drawn to pragmatist, poststructural, or postmodern arguments. Pragmatism would place traditional and modern views of authority, knowledge, and hierarchy in question. Critics might charge that pragmatist developments are "a sign of the sickness of our souls, a revolt against reason itself." I disagree. Poststructural and postmodern arguments pose challenges, to be sure. They present pragmatist opportunities as well.

Empiricism was part of what Rorty described as the linguistic turn. Several of the authors included in his volume—such as Moritz Schlick,

Rudolf Carnap, and Gustav Bergmann—were distinguished philosophers of empiricism. They attempted to account for the dramatic successes of modern science. One of their key assumptions was and remains remarkably appealing. It is that the stunning successes of modern science have been due to the fact that natural scientists had learned to speak correctly about the world. It is arguable that the intuitive reasonableness of this assumption is why empiricist and modernist sentiments remain strong today. The problem that the logical empiricists attempted to solve came directly from their assumption about the success of modern science: What is required if one is to speak correctly about the world? If this question could be answered, not only would it tell us how to go about describing and explaining the world but it would also guide our future experimentations with it.

The point of the linguistic turn, as Rorty remarked, was to answer this question either by reforming language, say, by bringing our systems of logic to higher levels of development, or by understanding more about the language we use, say, by uncovering what it is about ordinary language that enables us to cope successfully with the world, or both. Analytic philosophers possessed a paradigm. They had a series of relatively well-defined problems to solve. Or perhaps these problems were in possession of some very able philosophers.

That some people now use the term *postanalytic philosophy* indicates that somehow some philosophers have moved beyond or seek to move beyond the project of analytic philosophy. This could be because its goals have been achieved or because its central problems have been given up as beyond achievement (see Rajchman & West, 1985). Many, including myself, believe that it is the latter. Analytic philosophy always already contained elements of pragmatism and postanalytic philosophy. In parallel ways, this was also the case as structuralism transformed into post-structuralism and as modernism changed into postmodernism. Analytic philosophers defined their task rigorously. They, fortunately for us, took it very seriously. The result is that the passage from analytic to postanalytic philosophy is fairly clear, at least in broad outline. It is against this backdrop that the analyses of Quine and Davidson were produced. Their arguments clarify and place in relief the demise of structuralism and modernism as well.

It is not now possible to give a generalized account of what it means to speak correctly about the world; perhaps it will never be. The importance of this for educators is that if we cannot speak correctly about the world, then we cannot speak correctly about rationality, hierarchy, achievement, accountability, and literacy, for example, all of which constitute our educational and professional worlds. But how can this be? How can our ability to speak correctly about the world be questioned when apparently we do it successfully all day, every day?

Three assumptions have to be satisfied if one is to speak correctly about the world. The first has to do with what it means to speak "correctly." Correct speech was identified with logically valid speech.

> 1. There is a distinction between analytic and synthetic statements (this is the purported distinction between statements that make logically valid and truth-preserving arguments possible and empirical hypotheses that are tested against observations).

The second has to do with connecting speech to the world.

> 2. The meaning of theoretical terms is determined by a series of logical operations on those terms that reduce them to observable terms (this is variously known as reductionism or "operational definition").

The third assumes that we can distinguish speech about the world from the world itself.

> 3. There is a distinction between theoretical schemes (theories and descriptions of the world) and the content of those schemes (the world itself).

These assumptions seemed reasonable indeed, but they are presently notable more for their deconstruction than for their initial and intuitive appeal.

First, why is it important that analytic statements be distinct from synthetic statements? Why do empiricists require logically valid speech? What are the consequences—a pragmatist question for sure—of this assumption for educators? Richard Rudner (1966), an empiricist, defined a scientific theory as "a systematically related set of statements, including some lawlike generalizations, that is empirically testable" (p. 10). By "systematically related" Rudner meant that the logical structure of a theory should constitute a valid deductive argument. Not only should theories not be self-contradictory, at minimum, but they should be so constructed that if the axioms (premises) of the theory are true then the theorems (testable hypotheses) must also necessarily be true.

Analytic statements make truth-preserving arguments possible. They preserve the truths or meanings of the premises of a valid argument through to its conclusion. One aspect of correct speech, then, is the ability to preserve the truth of the premises to the conclusion of an argument. Synthetic statements, in contrast, are empirical generalizations. They are statements about the world. They are neither truth- nor meaning-preserving. Synthetic statements are empirical hypotheses that scientists test. They constitute the observational component of scientific theories. If empirical hypotheses are falsified, for example, and they are the conclusions of a logically valid theory, then one or some first principles and axioms of the theory will be falsified (see Popper, 1959). In this way, the empiricist account goes, scientists eventually can speak correctly about the world at a high level of abstraction and generality, perhaps at such a high level that its first principles would be "laws of nature."

Why is the analytic/synthetic distinction relevant to the day-to-day thoughts and activities of educators and educational researchers? Educational leaders and professionals acquire and assert authority in part because from time to time they claim to speak correctly about the world of schools and school systems. They are acceded a presumption of expertise. Imagine, for example, what might happen if educators were deprived of the authority that comes with the presumption of speaking Truth. If they cannot speak Truth, why should anyone listen to them? Why should they be respected? Why obeyed? In such circumstances education arguably reduces to coercion, manipulation, and influence. Put differently, the vacuum created by the inability to invoke educational Truths might be filled by unqualified and unchecked power. The issue at one level is Truth versus power. If we must give up Truth in thinking about our educational practices, then power stands ready to replace it as an ordering device. If the possibility of speaking correctly about schools is undermined or threatened, then we are (1) compelled to reinterpret what it means to possess authoritative knowledge about schools because (2) the traditional and modern conceptions of educational authority have become problematic. What follows is an extended argument for a pragmatist reinterpretation.

One important step is the deconstruction of the analytic/synthetic distinction. What follows, with perhaps excessive brevity, is W. V. O. Quine's investigation of the first and second assumptions listed above. Quine's strategy began with the clarification of the nature of analytic statements. He observed that there are two kinds of analytic statements. One type of analytic statement is a logical truth where, quoting Quine in his classic essay "Two Dogmas of Empiricism" (1953/1971), "in general a logical truth is a statement which is true and remains true under all reinterpretations of its components other than logical particles" (pp. 22–23). For example, the statement "No unmarried man is married" "remains true under any and all reinterpretations of 'man' and 'married'" (p. 22).

A second kind of analytic statement is exemplified by a statement such as "No bachelor is married" (p. 23). In the latter case, meaning is preserved when synonyms are substituted for synonyms. For example, if "unmarried man" is a synonym for "bachelor," then the meanings of "unmarried man" and "bachelor" are preserved when they are substituted for each other.

The problem of analyticity, as Quine called it, can be stated quite simply: How do we know or what would we have to know in order to determine that "unmarried man" and "bachelor" are synonyms? Our first inclination might be to appeal to a dictionary. Of course this tack is denied to us because dictionaries report *how words are used* (they are based on observations; they are synthetic statements) *not what words mean*. Synthetic statements cannot be used to establish the truth of analytic statements because we are trying to confirm just the opposite, that analytic and synthetic statements are distinct. After exploring many ways to solve the problem, Quine gave up, which turned out to be the point of his argument. He was unable to clearly characterize natural-language analyticity or synonymy, nor has anyone else since he first made this argument in the middle of the twentieth century.

With a little reflection, it is obvious that the problem of analyticity is a problem of *translation*. How is it possible *to translate* one word with another and be certain that the meaning of the first survives the substitution? If this question cannot be answered, a problem is created for empiricists and modernists that goes to the core of the project of rationally accumulating sure knowledge of the world. If this seemingly simple and rather obscure problem of translation cannot be solved, how can we hope to speak correctly about the world? Speaking continually demands that we substitute one word for another. If we do not know how to do this while retaining the meaning of the first word, then meanings, interpretations, translations, and metaphors are dispersed endlessly. Quine showed that the idea of "correct" speech is problematic before turning to the more involved question of how to speak correctly "about" the world.

The second dogma referred to in the title of Quine's essay is reductionism, that is more commonly called "operational definition" in textbooks and courses in research methodology. The dogma of reductionism directly addresses how to speak correctly about the world by asking how a word, such as *intelligence*, hooks onto the world by attaching itself to a specific and concrete manifestation of "intelligence." Here is how Quine described reductionism: "Every meaningful statement is held to be translatable into a statement (true or false) about immediate experience" (p. 38). After Quine demonstrated that the problem of analyticity reduces to synonymy, it is but a short step to understand that the issue of reductionism (operational definition) is also a matter of translation and synonymy. For example, if measures of mathematical achievement are not synonymous with the theoretical construct "mathematical achievement," then the empirical observations of what we record as mathematical achievement will not be identical with their theoretical counterparts. Consequently, our understanding of "mathematical achievement" may be misinformed. The issue is how to *translate* theoretical concepts into observations and vice versa. If clear conceptions of translation or synonymy do not exist, then research inferences remain problematic. Quine observed that "the two dogmas [the analytic/synthetic distinction and reductionism] are, indeed, at root identical" (p. 41). He continued: "My present suggestion is that it is nonsense, and the root of much nonsense, to speak of a linguistic component [analytic] and a factual component [synthetic] in the truth of any individual statement" (p. 42).

An important insight of Quine's argument is that *science is a rhetorical as well as a logical and evidentiary endeavor*; likewise with education. We are left to plead rhetorically for what we do because it is not possible to nail down once and for all that scientific (educational) theories are (1) truth- and meaning-preserving or (2) that our measurements of theoretical (educational) constructs capture our theoretical (administrative, curricular, instructional, policy) conceptions. We are left to argue for what we do and to hope that the conceivable practical consequences of our ideas turn out well. *Expertise, as a consequence (a pragmatic result), is rationalized in terms of its effects, not its Truth value.* When discourses of Truth and logic give way to discourses about effects and persuasion, the ideas of hierarchy, rationality, linear planning, and control also undergo interpretation and criticism. The pragmatist lesson of assessing results and outcomes in terms of art and aesthetics as we conduct worldly experiments in the midst of power returns. Arguments are sometimes called elegant or aesthetically pleasing but this often refers to formal characteristics such as parsimony, efficiency, scope, or power. When the natural language boundary between logic and rhetoric blurs, following Quine, the role of aesthetics in argumentation expands as well as becomes blurred itself. Quine's deconstruction of the analytic/synthetic distinction provides an opening for such an aesthetics. When natural language rules of proof are deferred we are required to make choices about desire. Where do we wish to go? How do we want to get there? These questions are necessarily aesthetic and cannot be wished away although effects of power often overwhelm and disguise such questions about beauty. As a result of his investigation, Quine observed that "one effect of abandoning [the analytic/synthetic distinction and reductionism] . . . is a shift toward pragmatism" (p. 20).[1]

A third assumption important to empiricists and modernists is the ability to distinguish between theoretical schemes and their content. This is known as the scheme/content distinction. It was the subject of Donald Davidson's presidential address to the Eastern Division of the American Philosophical Association. In his introductory comments, Davidson (1985) stated:

> Philosophers of many persuasions are prone to talk of conceptual schemes. Conceptual schemes, we are told, are ways of organizing experience; they are systems of categories that give form to the data of sensation; they are points of view from which individuals, cultures, or periods survey the passing scene. There may be no way of translating from one scheme to another, in which case the beliefs, desires, hopes, and bits of knowledge that characterize one person have no true counterparts for the subscriber to another scheme. Reality itself is relative to a scheme: what counts as real in one system may not in another. . . . Conceptual relativism is a heady and exotic doctrine, or would be if we could make good sense of it. The trouble is, as so often in philosophy, it is hard to improve intelligibility while retaining the excitement. At any rate that is what I shall argue. (p. 129)

Again, what is at stake? What are the conceivable consequences of deciding the question either way? If theories are not distinct from what they portray, then when they are tested they are, in part, tested against themselves. When this answer is generalized to education, the issue becomes important indeed. If we cannot safely assume a distinction between our conceptions and the world, then we cannot appeal to observations in order to ground decisively our scientific theories. If that is the case, then from where does educational authority—the authority to design, implement, or design curricula, for example—come? Here is the way Davidson put it:

> This . . . dualism of scheme and content, of organizing system and something waiting to be organized, cannot be made intelligible and defensible. It is itself a dogma of empiricism, the third dogma. The third, and perhaps the last, for if we give it up it is not clear that there is anything distinctive left to call empiricism. (p. 135)

Davidson came at the scheme/content question by investigating the problem of theory commensurability. How do we know if two different theories that appear to be different but claim to be about the same thing are or are not about the same "thing"? If our schemes and the world are distinct, it is possible that some schemes are incommensurable with other schemes, that is, we may have two or more schemes of the same world that cannot be translated from one to the other (again the issue of translation). Davidson argues that this is precisely what we do not and cannot know. If two or more schemes can be translated from one to another, then they are commensurable; but if two or more schemes cannot be translated from one to the other, then, quite simply, we do not know whether or not they are translatable from one to the other. The outcome is that we are required to remain agnostic about the existence of alternative conceptual schemes because we do not have access to a metascheme (a fixed scheme outside of our schemes), or metanarrative (an ultimate narrative by which other narratives can be definitively assessed), that enable us to make such judgments. Because we operate within a sea of textuality and not on firm land, as it were, we can never know whether we have one or many schemes.

Not knowing whether we have one scheme or many is one question, but distinguishing between scheme and content is another—or so it would seem. Davidson's response to the latter question is the same as to the previous one. The question is, How do we know whether the stories that we tell about the world result from the schemes we bring to the world or the way the world is? Or are our theories, explanations, schemes, stories, and narratives about the world grounded in an external reality (an important issue for empiricists)? Again, a metascheme or metanarrative is required in order to assess independently our schemes of the world and the world itself. Davidson argues that because we do not have such an Archimedean standpoint or decisive text outside of our immediate texts (a text outside of textuality, as Derrida might put it), then we must give up the scheme/content distinction. We do not know how to get outside of the schemes and narratives of our lives. When the scheme/content distinction goes, conceptual relativism and empiricism along with certain modernist pretensions go with it.

This argument generalizes easily to education. I return to the example of reading because educators are always reading. They are always already reading and writing the text of the situations with which they must deal. Fixed and final meanings of the texts that we read and write are constantly deferred. Scholes (1989) frames some of the complexity in a way that parallels Davidson's analysis:

> I have accepted the Derridean principle that there is no outside to textuality, but I have also said that the reader is always outside the text. This looks like confusion at worst and paradox at best, but it is neither. We are always outside any particular text we may attempt to read. This is why interpretation is a problem for us. But we are never outside the whole web of textuality in which we hold our cultural being and in which every text awakens echoes and harmonies. (p. 6)

But the texts that educators read are more involved than those described by Scholes. Educators are not always outside the texts they read. They are characters, as it were, within the texts that they read and interpret and write and edit. They must continually make a case for what they do and make a case without a "god's-eye view" of the situations with which they must deal. They do not have sure foundational knowledge from which to think and act. Educational theories and practices and experiences provide resources for arguing, making a case, and taking a stand. They do not provide final criteria or answers. Modernist conceptions of education highlight rationality, accountability, expertise, and control. Each of these is a textual production, however, that is used to generate yet other texts. When the scheme/content distinction goes, we are thrown back to conceptualizing and assessing the consequences of our beliefs and actions.

Connections between rhetoric and aesthetics can be seen in these arguments. Lacking foundational knowledge about schools and education, educators end up trying to tell each other and the public persuasive stories. Many stories can be persuasive. Each story has many meanings. Choices must be made. Not choosing is not an option because neither educators nor anyone else can function without operative texts. If they choose to parade the dominant stories about their profession and society without questioning them, then they, literally, are conduits for the efficient circulation of power. If they choose to interpret, criticize, and write the stories they tell, then they are artists. Assessing their art is a never-ending process.

The empiricist assumptions about analytic/synthetic and scheme/content distinctions and reductionism turned out to be unjustified. Ironically, they were exposed as metaphysical assumptions that were championed by scientists who sought to escape metaphysics. As a result, analytic philosophy and empiricism gave way to various forms of postanalytic philosophy and post-empiricism and to their close relatives, poststructuralism and postmodernism. Practices and orientations that were allies of these empiricist assumptions have turned out to have a long half-life for sure. Predicting the imminent demise of the residual influence of positivism and empiricism in education might not be accurate or wise. Modernist impulses that value control and accountability are likely to continue to support long-since-discredited positivist and empiricist myths.

I turn to program evaluation in the next chapter. While Quine and Davidson were constructing arguments that pointed away from the dogmas of empiricism, it is striking that empirical researchers were documenting repeated failures in attempts to manage change rationally.

CHAPTER 14

Pragmatism and The New Meaning of Educational Change

Developments in modern logic that were highlighted in the previous chapter contributed to a renewed interest in pragmatism. The numerous program evaluations of educational change studies that are reviewed in this chapter also contributed to pragmatism's revival. Evidence of the robustness of pragmatist ideas comes from the fact that academic philosophers and program evaluators, each speaking in their distinctive dialects and making their own authoritative arguments, came independently to pragmatist conclusions. There is no foundation for pragmatism, which is itself a pragmatist tenet. But the more persuasive stories we can tell from as many genres that we can draw upon that support pragmatist leanings and interpretations, the more credibility is lent to pragmatism (this, of course, is a pragmatist process itself). Now for a description of program evaluation leading to pragmatism.

Michael Fullan (1991) told a complex story of educational change. He described a thoroughly modern story of educational change research that initially advocated standards, accountability, control, productivity, and specialization. He showed in detail, however, that many actions carried out under the guise of modernization—my word, not his—have not been sufficiently effective to bring about the desired changes. This is a story about the limits of modernization in education. Likewise, it is a story about the value of pragmatism in education.

Fullan takes four tacks in addressing the meaning of change:

1. "the meaning of individual change in the society at large,"

2. "the *subjective* meaning of change for individuals,"

3. "description[s] of the *objective* meaning of change," and

4. "the implications of subjective and objective realities for understanding educational change" (p. 30).

As for 1 above, he quoted Marris (1975): "*All* real change involves loss, anxiety, and struggle" (Fullan, 1991, p. 31). Furthermore,

> Real change, then, whether desired or not, represents a serious personal and collective experience characterized by ambivalence and uncertainty. . . . The anxieties of uncertainty and the joys of mastery are central to the subjective meaning of educational change, and to success or failure—facts that have not been recognized or appreciated in most attempts at reform. (Fullan, 1991, p. 32)

A problem of educational change for teachers is that the subjective meaning of change (2 above) may not match policy descriptions of objective change (3 above). Huberman's (1983) discussion of classroom press illustrates this point. Classroom press includes the dictates of immediacy and concreteness, multidimensionality and simultaneity, adaptation to ever-changing conditions and unpredictability, and personal involvement with students. Classroom press also pushes for short-term perspectives, creates isolation from other adults, produces exhaustion, and provides limited opportunities for sustained reflection. When these characteristics of teaching are combined with "rational assumptions, abstraction, and descriptions of a proposed new curriculum . . . there is no reason for the teacher to believe in the change, and few incentives (and large costs) to find out whether a given change will turn out to be worthwhile" (Fullan, 1991, p. 34). The result, Fullan wrote, "has been two forms of nonchange: *false clarity* without change and *painful unclarity* without change" (p. 35, emphasis in original). He continued: "Ultimately the transformation of subjective realities [a discourse on one's thinking] is the essence of change" (p. 36).

The objective reality of educational change (3 above) is elusive. Fullan referred to Berger and Luckmann (1966) on the difficulty of defining objective "reality." There are two questions: (1) "What is the existing conception of reality on a given issue?" (2) "Says who?" (Berger & Luckmann, 1966, p. 116).[1] In responding to these questions, Fullan deconstructed an objective reality/subjective reality distinction by pointing out that objective realities are always already the product of (subjective) individual interpretations. He made a pragmatist move here as he acknowledged that different individuals trace out differently the "conceivable practical consequences" of the same practices and actions. He also argued that innovations and changes are multilayered. Some occur on the "surface" of things and others involve basic beliefs and identities.

The question of objective reality is complex because (1) each classroom innovation is multidimensional and multilayered and (2) each dimension and each layer of every innovation is open to multiple interpretations (a sociological echo of Quine and Davidson, Chapter 13, if you will). Additionally, there are interaction effects among people and policies:

> The real crunch comes in the relationships between these new programs or policies and the thousands of subjective realities embedded in people's individual and organizational contexts and their personal histories. How these subjective realities are addressed or ignored is crucial for whether potential changes become meaningful at the level of individual use and effectiveness. (Fullan, 1991, p. 43)

Fullan ultimately exposed and contested a subtext of many proposed educational changes. These subtexts are causal, although often ambiguous, hypotheses about how classrooms and schools work. They take this form: (1) Educational failures follow from the fact that our schools and educational systems are not sufficiently modern (efficient, rational, accountable). (2) If their premodern deficiencies—such as inefficiencies, lack of accountability, and incompetence—could be corrected, then our schools would be successful (what constitutes success remains ambiguous and is often only partially defined, at best).[2] There is another way of putting this: It is not that what educators have been doing is wrong-headed or inappropriate. The problem is that educators and educational reformers have not done well what they set out to do in the first place—create a modern educational system. After Fullan identified this subtext, he problematized it. Is it possible for teachers and other educators to become sufficiently modern and satisfy our educational desires? Is it possible to train, induce, cajole, reward, educate, or coerce teachers and other educators so that they will be rational, systematic, controlled, linear, and specialized enough *and* be willing to take the necessary risks to change schools in fundamental ways? Fullan says "no."

Fullan (1991) identified several constraints on attempts to rationalize change:

> It might be ... useful to accept the nonrational quality of social systems and move on from there. Patterson, Purkey, and Parker (1986) suggest that organizations in today's society do not follow an orderly logic, but a complex one that is often paradoxical and contradictory, but still understandable and amenable to influence. They contrast the assumptions of the rational conception with those of nonrational conception on five dimensions. *First*, goals: School systems are necessarily guided by multiple and sometimes competing goals. . . . *Second*, power: In school systems, power is distributed throughout the organization. *Third*, decision making: This is inevitably a bargaining process to arrive at solutions that satisfy a number of constituencies. *Fourth*,

external environment: The public influences school systems in major ways that are unpredictable. *Fifth,* teaching process: There are a variety of situationally appropriate ways to teach that are effective. (p. 97)

Plans are always subject to contingencies. Nonrational factors, then, are always already present in attempts to think and act rationally. Fullan's move away from rationalist assumptions can be said, broadly, to parallel Quine's and Davidson's move away from the dogmas of empiricism. Fullan repeatedly described limitations on rationality. Rational procedures, he documented, have a long history of failing to match up to the promises of educational change agents and reformers.

In his last chapter, Fullan advocated moving to new "paradigms" for educational change. Using the term *paradigm* may not be well advised here because paradigms imply modern solutions along with the normal, if not routinized, science that comes with them (Kuhn, 1972). Be that as it may, here are Fullan's (1991) six themes for the future of educational change.

> The six involve moving from an old, unsuccessful way of managing change to a new mind-set.
>   1. from negative to positive politics,
>   2. from monolithic to alternative solutions,
>   3. from innovations to institutional developments,
>   4. from going it alone to alliances,
>   5. from neglect to deeper appreciation of the change process, and
>   6. from "if only" to "if I" or "if we." (p. 347)

These themes are thoroughly pragmatic. They are forward-looking. They emphasize outcomes, multiple strategies and tactics, the institutional context within which the text of proposed changes is enacted, the role of community (alliances), and the importance of interpretation and criticism. The first move (1 above) is from a negative politics that imposes change from above and resistance from below to a positive politics of implementing a few principles. The move from monolithic to alternative solutions (2 above) rejects universal rationalistic solutions that are quintessentially modern. Monolithic solutions marginalize the contexts of change and limit one's flexibility in responding to the contingencies of the change process. This exemplifies what pragmatists believe about plurality. Richard Bernstein put it this way: "There can be no escape from plurality—a plurality of traditions, perspectives, philosophic orientations" (1989, p. 10).

A central motif is that we should *avert our gaze from the text* of an innovation and *look at the context of the institution* (3 above).[3] Changing emphasis from innovation to institution, perhaps, is Fullan's most overtly pragmatic recommendation. He asks us to look at the social and physical context of change as well as at the plurality of interests and visions of those involved. A shortsighted concern with innovation may obscure the point that successful change often requires institutional change. Fullan (1991) put it like an experimental pragmatist:

> Instead of tracing specific policies and innovations, we turn the problem on its head, and ask what does the array of innovative possibilities look like, if we are on the receiving or shopping end [as might an artist contemplating the reaction of a patron]. Thus institutional development . . . is the generic solution needed. Taking on one innovation at a time is fire fighting and faddism. Institutional development of schools and districts increases coherence and capacity for sorting out and integrating the myriad of choices, acting on them, assessing progress, and (re)directing energies. . . . We cannot develop institutions without developing the people in them. (p. 349)

This is comparable to the way pragmatists read and deconstruct the distinction between text and context. Furthermore, if (1) our theories and plans are fallible, (2) we lack foundational guidelines by which to make definitive judgments about what is true or false, and (3) we wish to be successful in what we attempt, then (4) it is better to be inclusive instead of exclusive by inviting others to participate in our deliberations and actions, thereby (5) making it possible to draw upon their knowledge and insights.[4]

Seymour Sarason (1990) made a similar point in *The Predictable Failure of Educational Reform.* He asks: For whom do schools exist? Repeatedly the answer given is that schools are for children. Sarason wrote: "If you, as I have, ask teachers . . . how they justify the existence of their school, the answer you get is that schools exist to further the intellectual and social development of students" (p. 137). This belief underlies school reform that emphasizes the text of a reform at the expense of context.

Sarason *rejects* the idea that schools exist *solely* for students.

> If . . . it is virtually impossible to create and sustain over time conditions for productive learning for students when they do not exist for teachers, the benefits sought by educational reform stand little chance of being realized. (p. 145).

Sarason's observation in benefit/cost terms is that whatever is changed, if it is to be sustained, must be perceived to be to everyone's advantage. Enduring change requires that everyone—students, teachers, administrators, staff, parents—believe that they benefit from the change, that it

produces net benefits for them. Otherwise, there is no incentive to perpetuate it. It is not likely that everyone—students, teachers, administrators,
others—will have the same self-described interests and desires. Different
participants will likely value the same outcomes differently. Therefore
negotiating change is required. Educational reformers who are caught up
in modernist conceptions of rationality, progress, and control may not
pay sufficient attention to context. Modernist ideas (the innovation) can
thereby become incapacitating straightjackets because they do not anticipate conceivable practical consequences.

This theme carries into Fullan's next point—"from going it alone to
alliances" (4 above). But here the argument takes a unexpected detour—
unexpected in terms of his previous observations. Instead of citing, say,
Dewey on democracy, Fullan introduced the idea of interactive professionalism. But the idea of an interactive professionalism suggests an underlying tension, if not contradiction, in his position. If nothing else, professionalism is a most modern conception. It appeals to expertise, control,
hierarchy, accountability, and rationality. Furthermore, his discussion of
professionalism fails to address how power operates through professional
structures and subjectivities (see Cherryholmes, 1988). Professionalism
and a focus on innovation have produced victories in contemporary education but also, as Fullan amply demonstrated, they have severely limited
and inhibited what can be done. There are good reasons to believe that
more professionalism is not the cure for the failures of professionalism
(after Havel, quoted in Chapter 11).

Successful change often requires one to embrace contradiction and
inconsistency (5 above):

> Change is difficult because it is riddled with dilemmas, ambivalences, and
> paradoxes. It combines steps that seemingly do not go together: to have a
> clear vision and be open-minded; to take initiative and empower others; to
> provide support and pressure; to start small and think big; to expect results
> and be patient and persistent; to have a plan and be flexible; to use top-down
> and bottom-up strategies; to experience uncertainty and satisfaction. (Fullan,
> 1991, p. 350)

But paradoxes, dilemmas, contradictions, and ambiguity subvert modern
impulses to linearity, control, and clarity. The modern and postmodern
exist together. What is modern, such as modernist proposals for educational change, is simultaneously accepted and rejected, utilized and criticized, appropriated and discarded by pragmatists.

Fullan's (1991) last suggestion broke with modern conceptions of
change in yet another way. He argued against relying on causal hypothe-

ses (6 above). He insisted that we should be wary of basing change on "if–then" thinking. The point is that the best chances for change exist when the change efforts have personal meaning for the individuals involved: "Acting on change is an exercise in pursuing meaning" (p. 351). This brings us full circle to Peirce's pragmatic maxim, whereby individuals find meaning by tracing conceivable practical consequences. For Fullan successful change requires "pursuing meaning" by way of a discourse on the consequences of thinking.

The modern and postmodern come together, then move apart in pragmatist attempts to bring about change. *Fullan's story ends in an assortment of paradoxes.* Here are a few:

1. Rational attempts to bring about change are likely to be enhanced when they incorporate irrational commitments.
2. Hierarchies that promote change are likely to improve their chances of success when the hierarchy itself is subverted.
3. Coordinated efforts to bring about change often depend for their success on uncoordinated responses to the complexities and inconsistencies of specific situations.
4. Impersonal goals are more likely to be achieved when they are personalized.

Fullan (1991) wrote:

> The only solution [to the problem of bringing about change] is that the whole school—all individuals—must get into the change business; if individuals do not do this, they will be left powerless. The current school organization is an anachronism. It was designed for an earlier period for conditions that no longer hold. It constrains the creation of a new profession of teaching that is so badly needed. Massive effort is required but it must come from individuals putting pressure on themselves and those around them. (p. 353)

This is an eloquent plea for pragmatism. Quine concluded "Two Dogmas of Empiricism" with an explicit turn to pragmatism. Fullan concluded *The New Meaning of Educational Change* with an implicit turn to pragmatism. In each case, as different as they are, the limitations of logic, rational planning and intervention, and modernity were highlighted. What are we left with? We are left to be experimental artists as we struggle and play together.

Reading Pragmatism: A Reprise

Pragmatist meanings are constructed. This idea is central to Peirce's maxim and to the naturalized epistemology of Dewey and Quine that followed. Here is how Quine put it: "I am of that large minority or small majority who repudiate the Cartesian dream of a foundation for scientific certainty firmer than scientific method itself. . . . I call the pursuit naturalized epistemology" (1992, p. 19). One point of naturalized epistemology and of the investigation of consequences is that they occur in natural settings, in context. Context can be a general text that sheds light on a specific text or it can be the material, social, and political conditions within which something exists or both. In interpreting the meaning of an object, such as an intellectual concept or professional practice, Scholes (1985) wrote: "I wish to argue that we can interpret it best only by taking our eyes off it, denying it status as a thing in itself, and reading it as intertextually as we can within the limits of the present discourse" (p. 136). Literary and physical contexts are not distinct from each other because the literary continually interprets the physical and the physical impinges upon the literary. Pragmatist meanings are products of both.

Tracing consequences can be thought of as the present looking forward. And the present itself is a construction of past experiments. A history of the present, therefore, is contextually important in imagining outcomes. As individuals we are who we are because of our location in multiple arenas; some are historical, some are literary, and some are social and political. What we can conceive is simultaneously made available and constrained by such factors.

The construction of conceptions and conjectures is not policed or authorized or detailed as might be done by foundational guidelines or a rule book. There is no revealed text, sacred or secular, that unambiguously and without interpretation discloses how things will turn out. To be sure, such revelations would solve the problem of inductive inference and take the guesswork out of conjecturing outcomes. Such a god's-eye view of the world would know these things, but to arrogate such knowledge to humans is secularly foolhardy and religiously blasphemous. It would mean that either we have obtained certain and sure knowledge of the world in the face of insufficient evidence and no proof or that we know the mind of god. Both mistakes are avoided when we take the linguistic turn and concede that all texts—including those that pretend to be foundational, scientific or religious—demand interpretation and criticism.

Interpretations permeate and constitute our goals, desires, and knowledge of the world. Everyone interprets. They do so from their unique positions and situations. Our positionality, as it were, coexists with our ethnocentrism, and it is useless to wish to escape either because that would require us to live outside of context. Many interpretations are wrong-headed and useless fictions, but many are creative and productive in imagining and contributing to desirable outcomes. Plural interpretations have evolutionary survival value because some of them suggest how in our endless experimentation we can profitably interact with the world and each other. Conjectures, images, and conceptualizations are not equally beautiful or useful. Because we do not have decisive texts that distinguish clearly the better from the worse, we must choose among them, and we cannot deny the responsibility for our choices.[1] Pragmatist *realism* results from the fact that our choices are not equally efficacious or desirable and from the fact that pragmatists are interested in outcomes. Because pragmatists are interested in consequences, they are prevented from wishing their way through life. Pragmatists are realists who do not have access to Truth.

Pleasure or pain? Or pain or pleasure? Which shall we choose? The easy answer is to choose pleasure. Easy answers are often elusive. The pleasure/pain distinction, for example, deconstructs. Shall we choose to watch a basketball game (immediate pleasure) or sit at a personal computer in order to finish a manuscript (short-term pain perhaps, but long-term pleasure)? Are we to reward students in a classroom (short-term pleasure possibly for students and teacher) even though they did not complete their assignment—by failing to finish, say, a lesson on fractions (long-term pain for the students perhaps)—or demand more of them (short-term coercion and pain), thus leading to a greater command of fractions (long-term pleasure)? As ideas about pleasure, beauty, satisfaction, and fulfillment are translated into specific situations, the pragmatist as calculator meets and accedes to the pragmatist as artist. Pragmatism as calculation serves pragmatism as art because only after decisions have been made about what constitutes satisfaction (on which dimensions do you wish to be highly ranked?) do calculations become relevant. This is another example of values taking precedence over facts.

The pragmatist as artist cannot escape, it seems, from the fact that she is both effect and cause of her community. She learns from her community what and how to produce what is desirable. Her productions, in turn, shape her community's desires as the circulation of power produces and reproduces her community and society (see Giddens, 1979, for his discussion of structuration). Because we cannot escape the texts that constitute our lives, then, it is to our advantage to be good, very good readers. If we are either efficient or slapdash in reproducing texts—whether they are of power, knowledge, or art—then we act to reproduce the world that has been anonymously dictated to us.

We are caught in the flow and content of power as it happens to find us. Power substitutes many times for authoritative foundational texts that we do not have. But the effects and texts of power, even as they are routinized and institutionalized in modern professions, deconstruct. The texts of power have gaps. Textual gaps are important resources because they provide openings for interpretation and criticism that undercut domination and repetition. This provides opportunities for expansive and unorthodox experimentation.

The artfulness that pragmatists pursue is constructed in the midst of both power and incomplete and uncertain knowledge. Pragmatism can be thought of as a postmodern dance among art, power, and knowledge that engenders thought and action. Substantive and specific interpretation and criticism give content to how they are and can be choreographed. Solidarity as we sharpen our reading skills in collectively negotiating and tracing consequences promises a future where we might arguably—it repeatedly comes back to what can be imagined, said, and pursued—be better artists of ordinary experience.

Pragmatists on Pragmatism

It may be the case that all that pragmatism can be is found in Peirce's pragmatic maxim. But the pragmatic maxim can be read in many ways. I offer the following interpretations of pragmatism by various pragmatists, famous and not so famous, to display this variability and to offer a contrast to my reading of pragmatism.

CHARLES SANDERS PEIRCE

In a proper sense pragmatism begins with Charles Sanders Peirce, who formulated some of its major ideas in his 1878 essay, "How to Make Our Ideas Clear."[1] Here is his 1878 statement of the pragmatic maxim:

> Consider what effects which might conceivably have practical bearings we conceive the object of our conception to have. Then, our conception of these effects is the whole of our conception of that object. (1878/1989, p. 88)

This statement seems unnecessarily complicated, to me at least, especially for a principle that was formulated to help us clarify the meaning of our concepts. Here is his 1905 version of the maxim.

> The method prescribed in the [pragmatic] maxim is to trace out in the imagination the conceivable practical consequences—that is, the consequences for deliberate, self-controlled conduct—of the affirmation or denial of the concept; and the assertion of the maxim is that herein lies the *whole* of the purport of the word, the *entire* concept. (1905/1984, p. 493, emphasis in original)

John Murphy on Peirce

John Murphy (1990) summarized what he called Peircean pragmatism in the following series of points.

1. Beliefs are identical if and only if they give rise to the same habit of action. (p. 25)

113

2. Beliefs give rise to the same habit of action if and only if they appease the same doubt by producing the same rule of action. (p. 25)

3. The meaning of a thought is the belief it produces. (p. 26)

4. Beliefs produce the same rule of action only if they lead us to act in the same sensible situations. (p. 26)

5. Beliefs produce the same rule of action only if they lead us to the same sensible results. (p. 26)

6. There is no distinction of meaning so fine as to consist in anything but a possible difference in what is tangible and conceivably practical. (p. 26)

7. Our idea of anything is our idea of its sensible effects. (p. 27)

8. Consider what effects, that might conceivably have practical bearings, we conceive the object of our conception to have. Then our conception of these effects is the whole of our conception of the object. (the pragmatic maxim, p. 27)

8a. Ask what are our criteria for calling a thing P. Then our conception of those criteria is the whole of our conception of P-ness (P-ity, P-hood, . . .). (p. 28)

9. A true belief is one which is fated to be ultimately agreed to by all who investigate scientifically. (Peirce's theory of truth, p. 31)

10. Any object represented in a true belief is real. (p. 31) (Peirce's principle of meaning) If one can define accurately all the criteria governing uses to which a predicate can be put, one will have therein a complete definition of the meaning that it predicates. (p. 46)

WILLIAM JAMES

William James, a close friend and benefactor of Peirce, was one of the classic pragmatists in the late nineteenth and early twentieth century. Here is a story that he told in a famous lecture to convey the meaning of pragmatism.

> Some years ago, being with a camping party in the mountains, I returned from a solitary ramble to find every one engaged in a ferocious metaphysical dispute. The *corpus* of the dispute was a squirrel—a live squirrel supposed to be clinging to one side of a tree-trunk; while over against the tree's opposite side a human being was imagined to stand. This human witness tries to get sight of the squirrel by moving rapidly round the tree, but no matter how

fast he goes, the squirrel moves as fast in the opposite direction, and always keeps the tree between himself and the man, so that never a glimpse of him is caught. The resultant metaphysical problem now is this: *Does the man go around the squirrel or not?* He goes round the tree, sure enough, and the squirrel is on the tree; but does he go round the squirrel? . . . Everyone had taken sides, and was obstinate; and the numbers of both sides were even. Each side, when I appeared, appealed to me to make it a majority. Mindful of the scholastic adage that whenever you meet a contradiction you must make a distinction, I immediately sought and found one, as follows: "Which party is right," I said, "depends on what you *practically* mean by 'going round' the squirrel. If you mean passing from the north of him to the east, then to the south, then to the west, and then to the north of him again, obviously the man does go round him, for he occupies these successive positions. But if on the contrary you mean being first in front of him, then on the right of him, then behind him, then on his left, and finally in front again, it is quite as obvious that the man fails to go round him, for by the compensating movements the squirrel makes, he keeps his belly turned towards the man all the time, and his back turned away. Make the distinction and there is no occasion for any farther dispute. You are both right and both wrong according as you conceive the verb 'to go round' in one practical fashion or the other.

This trivial anecdote . . . is a peculiarly simple example of what I wish now to speak of as *the pragmatic method.* . . . The pragmatic method . . . interpret[s] each notion by tracing its respective practical consequences. What difference would it practically make to any one if this notion rather than that notion were true? If no practical difference whatever can be traced, then the alternatives mean practically the same thing, and all dispute is idle. . . . To attain perfect clearness in our thoughts of an object, then, we need only consider what conceivable effects of a practical kind the object may involve— what sensations we are to expect from it, and what reactions we must prepare. (1907/1981, pp. 25–26)

Here is James's characterization of what he called the pragmatic method in "What pragmatism means" (1907/1981):

The pragmatic method means *looking away from first things, principles, 'categories,' supposed necessities; and looking towards last things, fruits, consequences, facts.* (p. 29; emphasis in original).

John Murphy on James

John Murphy (1990) summarized James's pragmatic conception of truth and other elements of his pragmatism with the following:

1. What is true in our way of thinking is what is expedient on the whole and in the long run. (p. 55)

2. What is expedient on the whole and in the long run in our way of thinking is the production of beliefs that are true. (p. 56)

3. The beliefs that prove themselves to be good, and good for definite, assignable reasons, are the true ones. (p. 56)

4. What is true in our way of thinking is the production of beliefs that prove themselves to be good, and good for definite, assignable reasons. (James's theory of truth, p. 57)

5. If one can define accurately all the possible worlds and possible lives in which a sentence is true, one will have therein a complete account of the credibility of what the sentence says. (James's principle of credibility, p. 47)

6. An idea is true instrumentally just insofar as it helps us to get into satisfactory relations with other parts of our experience. (James's definition of a technical term, p. 51)

7. An idea is becoming true if and only if it is true instrumentally. (James's definition of an idea becoming true instrumentally, p. 51)

JOHN DEWEY

Pragmatism . . . presents itself as an extension of historical empiricism, but with this fundamental difference, that it does not insist upon antecedent phenomena but upon consequent phenomena; not upon precedents but upon the possibilities of action. And this change in point of view is almost revolutionary in its consequences. An empiricism which is content with repeating facts already past has no place for possibility and for liberty (Dewey, 1931/ 1989, p. 33).

H. S. THAYER

1. A maxim or procedural principle in philosophy and science for explicating the meanings of certain concepts.

2. A theory of knowledge, experience, and reality maintaining: (a) that thought and knowledge are biologically and socially evolved modes of adaptation to and control over experience and reality; (b) that reality possesses a transitional character and that thought is a guide to the realization and satisfaction of our interests and purposes; that all knowledge is evaluative of future experiences and consequences of actions—thus in organizing conditions of future observations and experience. Thought is a behavioral process manifested in controlled actualizations of selected, anticipated and planned possibilities of future experience.

It remains only to append one further note to the survey in order to bring the contents up to date.

3. In recent literature under the influence of Dewey and Lewis as well as F. P. Ramsey, Rudolf Carnap, Ernest Nagel, W. V. O. Quine, et al., "pragmatism" connotes one broad philosophic attitude toward our conceptualization of experience: theorizing over experience is, as a whole and in detail, fundamentally motivated and justified by conditions of efficacy and utility in serving our various aims and needs. The ways in which experience is apprehended, systematized, and anticipated may be many. Here pragmatism counsels tolerance and pluralism. But, aside from esthetic and intrinsic interests, all theorizing is subject to the critical objective of maximum usefulness in serving our needs. Our critical decisions in general will be pragmatic, granted that in particular cases decisions over what is most useful or needed in our rational endeavors are relative to some given point of view or purposes.

The three parts of this outline comprise a general definition of pragmatism. (Thayer, 1984, p. 431)

RICHARD RORTY

"Pragmatism" is a vague, ambiguous, and overworked word. Nevertheless, it names the chief glory of our country's intellectual tradition. . . . (1982, pp. 160, 165–166)

My first characterization of pragmatism is that it is simply anti-essentialism applied to notions like "truth," "knowledge," "language," "morality," and similar objects of philosophical theorizing. (1982, p. 162)

[A] second characterization of pragmatism might go like this: there is no epistemological difference between truth about what ought to be and truth about what is, nor any metaphysical difference between facts and values, nor any methodological difference between morality and science. . . . For the pragmatists, the pattern of all inquiry—scientific as well as moral—is deliberation concerning the relative attractions of various concrete alternatives. The idea that in science or philosophy we can substitute "method" for deliberation between alternative results of speculation is just wishful thinking. (1982, pp. 163, 164)

[A] third and final characterization of pragmatism . . . is that there are no constraints on inquiry save conversational ones—no wholesale constraints derived from the nature of the objects, or of the mind, or of language, but only those retail constraints provided by the remarks of our fellow inquirers. The pragmatist . . . wants us to give up the notion that God, or evolution, or some other underwriter of our present world-picture, has programmed us as machines for accurate very picturing and that philosophy brings self-knowledge by letting us read our own program. . . . There is no method for knowing when one has reached the truth, or when one is closer to it than before. (1982, p. 166)

Our identification with our community—our society, our political tradition, our intellectual heritage—is heightened when we see this community as ours rather than nature's, shaped rather than found, one among many which men have made. In the end, the pragmatists tell us, what matters is our loyalty to other human beings clinging together against the dark, not our hope of getting things right. (1982, p. 166)

Pragmatists are supposed to treat everything as a matter of a choice of context and nothing as a matter of intrinsic properties. They dissolve objects into functions, essences into momentary foci of attention, and knowing into success at reweaving a web of beliefs and desires into more supple and elegant folds. (1985, p. 134)

STEVEN KNAPP AND WALTER BENN MICHAELS

The only point of pragmatism is the inseparability of practice and belief. (1985. p. 143)

From a pragmatist perspective, then, disagreements about language—or anything else—are always practical. (1985, p. 144)

JOSEPH MARGOLIS

Let us construe "pragmatism" as a term of art. We shall take any philosophy to be *pragmatist* to the extent that it distinctly favors three doctrines. It must, first, oppose foundationalism with respect to whatever cognitive powers it presupposes. Hence, the epistemological claims of Platonism, Cartesian and Kantian certainty, sense-datum theories, Husserlian reduction, totalized systems of the structuralist possibilities of any cultural or cognitive domain, the discovery of the "true" or "single" language of nature, even the discovery of the fixed laws of nature, are all precluded. Secondly, it must compensate for this first constraint by presupposing that, in a sense not epistemically privileged regarding the survival of the human species obtains: namely that our cognitive powers and our theories of those powers must be judged sufficiently grounded in reality for our sustained adherence to them not, as such, to entail the extinction or near-extinction, or related jeopardy of the human species. Thirdly, it must provide for the cognitive success of valid forms of inquiry in terms continuous with, and dependent upon, the conditions of social praxis—that is, the historically variable activities by which apparently viable societies intervene in nature and reproduce their kind. (1986, pp. 201–202)

RICHARD BERNSTEIN

Richard Bernstein's (1989) presidential address to the Eastern Division of the American Philosophical Association developed these characteristics of pragmatism.

1. Anti-foundationalism. (p. 7)

2. Their alternative to foundationalism was to elaborate a thoroughgoing fallibilism where we realize that although we must begin any inquiry with prejudgments and can never call everything into question at once, nevertheless there is no belief or thesis—no matter how fundamental—that is not open to further interpretation and criticism. (p. 8)

3. It is this fallibilism that brings me to the next theme that is so vital for the pragmatists—the social character of the self and the need to nurture a critical community of inquirers. (p. 9)

4. Anti-foundationalism, fallibilism, and the nurturing of critical communities leads to the fourth theme running through the pragmatic tradition—the awareness and sensitivity to radical contingency and chance that mark the universe, our inquiries, our lives. (p. 9)

5. I come finally to the theme of plurality. . . . There can be no escape from plurality—a plurality of traditions, perspectives, philosophic orientations. (p. 10)

C. G. PRADO

C. G. Prado (1989) characterized pragmatism on the basis of an earlier Philip Wiener essay (1973). Here are the key elements of Weiner's account and selections from Prado's explication of it.

Wiener attributes to pragmatism four central tenets: a pluralistic empiricism, a temporalistic view of reality, a contextualist conception of reality and values, and a secular democratic individualism. . . . [1] A pluralistic empiricism is first of all a rejection of a priorism, but without a corresponding doctrinaire commitment to "experience" as the sole source of knowledge. The point [of the latter qualification] is that pragmatism accepts a variety of accounts of knowledge and of the criteria for knowledge. . . . The heart of the pragmatic claim is that the criteria for knowledge are inherently societal and historical, and there can be no prior determination of it sources or limits. What counts as knowledge may change, as may what counts as justification for belief.

... [2] The temporalistic view of reality and knowledge, overlaps the first. ... This espousal of historicism rejects access to a determinate reality that somehow underlies, and grounds judgments about, the world, thereby rendering at least some of them ahistorical and foundational with respect to others. But note that reality is not at issue, only our access to it, and the coherence of the notion that an accessible reality, independent of our constructs, serves to ground judgments and beliefs. [3] This point leads to the third tenet, the contextualistic conception of reality and values, whose point is precisely that "reality" is what is counted as such in a particular historical context. . . . [This] is to say that we take to be real and of value what our time and place lead us to. . . . [4] The fourth tenet, secular democratic individualism . . . opposes the exclusion or subjugation of the individual in social and political realms on the basis of overriding principles, values, or objectives. By rejecting transcendent values or principles as grounds for institutional aims and practices, it rejects totalitarianism (1989, pp. 9–11).

NANCY FRASER

Begin with the sort of zero-degree pragmatism that is compatible with a variety of substantive political views, with socialist feminism as well as bourgeois liberalism. This pragmatism is simply anitessentialism with respect to traditional philosophical concepts like truth and reason, human nature and morality. . . . Then add the kind of zero-degree holism that combines easily with radical democratic politics. This holism is simply the sense of the difference between the frame of a social practice and a move within it. . . . Next, add a keen sense of the decisive importance of language in political life. Mix with the pragmatism and the holism until you get a distinction between making a political claim in a taken-for-granted vocabulary and switching to a different vocabulary. . . . Now, add a view of contemporary societies as neither hyperindividualized nor hypercommunalized. Contestation, in turn, should be broadly conceived to include struggle over cultural meanings and social identities, as well as over more narrowly traditional political stakes like electoral office and legislation. . . . This broad sense of contestation allows for a politics of culture that cuts across traditional divisions between public and private life. (1989, pp. 106–107)

CORNEL WEST

In the course of writing a book that sympathetically portrays pragmatism as "the American evasion of philosophy" Cornell West (1989) outlined his vision of prophetic pragmatism. The prophetic pragmatism of West is more concerned with the social processes and consequences of society than with the underlying assumptions of pragmatism.

The tradition of pragmatism . . . is in need of an explicit political mode of cultural criticism that refines and revises Emerson's concerns with power, provocation, and personality in light of Dewey's stress on historical consciousness and Du Bois' focus on the plight of the wretched of the earth. . . . Prophetic pragmatism, with its roots in the American heritage and its hopes for the wretched of the earth, constitutes the best chance of promoting an Emersonian culture of creative democracy by means of critical intelligence and social action. The first step is to define what an Emersonian culture of creative democracy would look like, or at least give some sense of the process by which it can be created. (1989, p. 212)

To speak then of an Emersonian culture of creative democracy is to speak of a society and culture where politically adjudicated forms of knowledge are produced in which human participation is encouraged and for which human personalities are enhanced. Social experimentation is the basic norm, yet it is operative only when those who must suffer the consequences have effective control over the institutions that yield the consequences, i.e., access to decision-making processes. . . . The Emersonian swerve from epistemology is inseparable from an Emersonian culture of creative democracy; that is there is political motivation and political substance to the American evasion of philosophy. (1989, p. 213)

The political substance of the American evasion of philosophy is that what was the prerogative of philosophers, i.e., rational deliberation, is now that of the people—and the populace deliberating is creative democracy in the making. . . . This view is not a license for eliminating or opposing all professional elites, but it does hold them to account. Similarly, the populace deliberating is neither mob rule nor mass prejudice. Rather, it is the citizenry in action, with its civil consciousness molded by participation in public-interest-centered and individual-rights-regarding democracy. Prophetic pragmatism makes this political motivation and political substance of the American evasion of philosophy explicit. Like Dewey, it understands pragmatism as a political form of cultural criticism and locates politics in the everyday experiences of ordinary people. (1989, p. 213)

Reading Pragmatism: An Outline

According to the *Oxford English Dictionary* the word *pragmatism* has Greek antecedents that mean "a deed, act." The *OED* gives the following as pragmatism's philosophical meaning

> The doctrine that the whole "meaning" of a conception expresses it-self in practical consequences either in the shape of conduct to be recommended, or of experiences to be expected, if the conception be true (W. James); or the method of testing the value of any asser-tion that claims to be true, by its consequences, i.e., by its practical bearing upon human interests and purposes (F. C. S. Schiller).

The political definition the *OED* gives of pragmatism is:

> Theory that advocates dealing with social and political problems primarily by practical methods adapted to the existing circum-stances, rather than by methods which have been conformed to some ideology.

As with most definitions, some aspects of the definiendum are captured but much complexity escapes without notice.

Charles Sanders Peirce first formulated what came to be known as the pragmatic maxim in an 1878 essay, "How to Make our Ideas Clear" (1878/1989) and revised it in this 1905 version.

> The method prescribed in the [pragmatic] maxim is to trace out in the imagina-tion the conceivable practical consequences—that is, the consequences for deliberate, self-controlled conduct—of the affirmation or denial of the concept; and the assertion of the maxim is that herein lies the *whole* of the purport of the word, the *entire* concept. (Peirce, 1905, 1984, p. 493)

Frank Macke, a contemporary pragmatist, expanded on Peirce's maxim when he wrote that "pragmatism is a discourse on the consequences of thinking" (1995, p. 158).[1] Pragmatists are interested in consequences of beliefs and actions, not altogether a simple task. What does it mean to be interested in consequences of beliefs and actions?

1. Pragmatists are interested in *conceivable practical consequences of affirming an idea or taking an action.*
2. Pragmatists are interested in *consequences that are satisfying and desirable.* They act as artists as they contemplate outcomes and critics as they assess them.
3. *Anticipating consequences occurs in a context of power* that shapes our conceptions and how we value them. Therefore, criticism includes assessing the exercise and effects of power. (It should be noted that American (U.S.) pragmatists have not always appreciated or highlighted the material and political construction of and constraint on desires, conceptions, and inquiry. This is evidence for the limits imposed by ethnocentrism [context] as well as the insights it [ethnocentrism] offers, which, pragmatists argue, shape us all.)
4. Because pragmatism is anticipatory and forward-looking, it is inductive. Therefore, *pragmatists are fallibilists.* Unless the future is like the past *and* we know the past completely and correctly, whatever we anticipate may be in error. Pragmatists expect that even our most deeply held beliefs may someday need revision.
5. Criticism and inquiry are material as well as a social processes. They are subject to influences that are apprehended and acknowledged and unapprehended and unacknowledged. The social construction of reality that we acquire en route to becoming members of society favors some understandings and explanations and actively silences or passively ignores others. Therefore, when pragmatists assess, estimate, and project consequences, *they are also social and cultural critics.*
6. Because pragmatists are interested in consequences and not in discovering Truth once and for all time, it follows that *they cannot be skeptical* when final Truths about the world are not forthcoming. Skepticism is dependent upon and intimately related to the search for Truth; when one gives up the search for Truth (when the Truth/No Truth distinction deconstructs), skepticism goes with it. If one believes that it is always possible that beliefs about the world can be wrong, there is no reason to be surprised when beliefs turn out to be erroneous; of course, it is possible to be surprised about which beliefs are wrong. Pragmatists also recognize that they can be wrong because of
7. The *contingency* of the world. The world seems to be continually changing and evolving, and we have no final handle, it is arguable, on what is going on today much less what will happen tomorrow. Therefore,

8. Pragmatists are *anti-essentialists.* They do not believe that there are essences—say, of education, intelligence, water, mass, truth, rationality, or justice. God may know all things, but a god's-eye view of the world is useless to us because, as people, we have purposes and points of view. If from a human perspective there are only points of view and no essences, it follows that

9. Pragmatists are *anti-representationlists.* If there are no essential properties of the world, then there is nothing definitive about the world to "represent." There are purposes and consequences and getting by, but nothing final to say because the world can be described differently from different perspectives. There is neither a beginning nor an end to the pragmatist discourse. It then follows that

10. Pragmatists are *anti-foundationalists.* Pragmatists are interested in speaking effectively but not correctly about the world.[2] Because pragmatists are continually caught up in an inductive, inferential, and artistic process, they are not concerned with foundational principles that would guarantee claims to truth, rationality, objectivity, or progress. In this sense pragmatists are interested in a naturalized epistemology, that is, in ways of knowing that are contextually circumscribed.

11. Pragmatists, as a result, are *contextualists.* They eagerly deconstruct the distinction between the texts of their beliefs and actions and the contexts within which those texts are enacted. This is another result of the fact that the consequences of thinking and acting cannot be limited a priori. In methodological terms, pragmatists assume that interaction effects constantly mediate among the texts and contexts of their beliefs.

12. Because pragmatists are continually engaged in fallibilistic inductive exercises, there is always the possibility that some consequence that was initially overlooked will later prove to be of decisive importance. It is reasonable, then, to think as broadly as possible when considering the consequences of beliefs and actions. Related, then, to rejecting a text/ context distinction is the fact that pragmatists are *holistic* in their thinking. They reject distinctions such as: fact/value, objective/subjective, theory/ practice, ends/means, rational/irrational, analytic/synthetic, and scheme/ content. As contextualists and holists,

13. Pragmatists emphasize the importance of *community* because they recognize that an individual's subjectivity and desires are continually formed in the context of and in interaction with others.

14. Pragmatists are *socially inclusive* in their conception of community and extend the scope of one's community as far as possible because those who are different from oneself, who speak from different points of view and provide alternative descriptions, might identify previously unfore-

seen and disastrous or, perhaps, beneficial and beautiful consequences of beliefs and actions. Pragmatists wish to extend the conception of *us* as far as possible.

15. For these same reasons, pragmatists wish to live in democracies where a wide range of viewpoints are likely to be expressed, thereby enriching the "discourse on the consequences of thinking." Authoritarian limits on inquiry are *necessarily* unpragmatic. Because of their inclusiveness and commitment to democracy, pragmatists ascribe to the tenet:

16. *Do not block inquiry.* Pragmatist inquiry continually reweaves our web of beliefs and tastes.

17. *Open communication is important* because desires, conceptions, and inquiry are products of, among other things, communication with others. In an effort to identify individual and social pathologies and to broaden the scope of choice, pragmatists place high value on

18. *Education.* Education broadens our conceptions and our discourses about their consequences, and it illuminates our choices about society and how to live.

19. Pragmatists, obviously, are interested in consequences that contribute to the *survival of the species* (they choose survival over extinction); otherwise there are no consequences to contemplate.

20. The result (a pragmatist outcome) is that as we anticipate consequences of beliefs and actions, *we choose our society and way of life.*

Notes

CHAPTER 1

1. Instead of anticipating consequences, positivists and empiricists sought to give an account of the towering achievements of modern science. They attempted to produce an account of objective knowledge that would be defensible against all criticism. They were not interested in anticipating consequences, or, perhaps, they were interested in anticipating consequences but only as a result of finding first principles. In any case, they hoped to contribute to the rationalization of social practices, including education, by escaping the dominant metaphysical assumptions of Western thought. Theirs was a compelling project, and one of its effects was a lack of interest in pragmatism.

2. The discussion of aesthetics in Chapter 1 and the expansive reading of practical consequences in Chapter 2 illustrate that I give a very broad definition to practical consequences. The practicality of a consequence depends on for whom the outcome is consequential.

3. Frank Lentricchia's (1990) "In Place of an Afterword—Someone Reading" was suggestive for consciously approaching pragmatism as something to be read.

4. There are many readings of pragmatism. Many of their differences are due to what Phyllis Rooney (1993) calls disparate "interpretations of the key notion of 'practical consequences'" (p. 22). Alternative interpretations include Nancy Fraser's (1989), that outlines a feminist view, as does Charlene Haddock Seigfried's (1993). Then there is Cornel West's prophetic one (West, 1989), the pragmatist glimmerings in Jacques Derrida's account of deconstruction (Derrida, 1996), and John Stuhr's (1997) genealogical pragmatism, that also connects with French postmodernist thought. We find a liberal discursive view in Richard Rorty's (1979, 1982) work and an aesthetic explication and extension in Richard Shusterman's (1992, 1997) writing. Jim Garrison has expanded on various implications of Dewey's aesthetics (Garrison, 1995, 1997) for teaching and education. Of course, there is John Dewey's formidable account(s) of pragmatism that was (were) broadly aesthetic as well as democratic (see Dewey, 1934/1980 for only a start). This listing is not exhaustive by any means.

CHAPTER 3

1. Richard Rorty, perhaps more than anyone else, has revived interest in pragmatism with *Philosophy and the Mirror of Nature* (1979), *The Consequences of Pragmatism*

(1982), *Objectivity, Relativism, and Truth,* and *Essays on Heidegger and Others* (1991). In addition, see Joseph Margolis, *Pragmatism Without Foundations: Reconciling Realism and Relativism* (1986); C. G. Prado, *The Limits of Pragmatism* (1987); Giles Gunn, *Thinking Across the American Grain: Ideology, Intellect, and the New Pragmatism* (1992); and David Hall, *Richard Rorty: Prophet and Poet of the New Pragmatism* (1994).

In education my 1988 book *Power and Criticism: Poststructural Investigations in Education* approached pragmatism from the perspective of poststructural thought. In addition, see Tom Skrtic, *Behind Special Education: A Critical Analysis of Professional Culture and School Organization* (1991); Spencer Maxcy *Educational Leadership: A Critical Pragmatic Perspective* (1991) and *Democracy, Chaos, and the New School Order* (1995); William Stanley, *Curriculum for Utopia: Social Reconstructionism and Critical Pedagogy in the Postmodern Era* (1992); and Jim Garrison, *Dewey and Eros: Wisdom and Desire in the Art of Teaching* (1997) and *The New Scholarship on Dewey* (1995).

2. This is not a history of pragmatism, for which I defer to other excellent histories and commentaries. Some of the more distinguished include H. S. Thayer, *Meaning and Action: A Critical History of Pragmatism* (1981); Cornel West, *The American Evasion of Philosophy: A Genealogy of Pragmatism* (1989); and John Murphy, *Pragmatism: From Peirce to Davidson* (1990).

3. William James, in his 1907 essay "What Pragmatism Means" (1907/1975, p. 26), interpreted *pragma* as "action." I thank Richard Zinmantor for help with these translations.

4. In a famous lecture William James demonstrated how the pragmatic method could be used to clarify meaning by telling a story about a squirrel. This story is excerpted in the Appendix A.

5. Rooney (1993) puts it like this.

> Peirce's emphasis is much more positivistic than James's or Dewey's. His emphasis is on correct methodology, on establishing the meaning of terms with "practical consequences" that turn out for the most part to be the "sensible effects" of (preferably scientific circumscribed) action and observation. . . . James and Dewey recognized that there are important dimensions of our full experience that are not necessarily reducible to ostensible action and sensible effect yet have "practical consequences" on our lives. (p. 22)

6. I will occasionally use the phrase "pragmatists believe." But pragmatists believe a lot of different things and disagree on many of them. When I use this phrase I am only claiming that the view that I am stating is pragmatist in nature and that some other pragmatist, somewhere, might agree with it. Pragmatism is not an ideology and, as will become clear, it can be elaborated in seemingly endless ways.

CHAPTER 4

1. Increasing attention was paid to the place of aesthetics in pragmatism during the last decades of the twentieth century. Jim Garrison wrote that a major theme

in new scholarship on John Dewey was "the tendency to place Dewey's aesthetics at the center of his thinking instead of his theory of inquiry, theory of democratic social relations, or even his philosophy of education" (1995, p. 1). See also Garrison (1997), Shusterman (1992, 1997), and Alexander (1987).

2. Given the proliferation of categorical distinctions in contemporary discourse, one might be tempted to treat aesthetics as distinct from ethics and power. I reject this. They pervasively accompany and infect each other. Aesthetics and ethics can be substituted for power in the following description of Foucault's work by Susan Bickford: "For Foucault, power is not something we can abdicate or avoid. Even in our resistance, we create and perpetuate relations of power. (In freeing ourselves from one oppression, we may in fact be enacting another unforseen oppression.)" (1993, p. 115). So it is with our conceptions of value, beauty, and desire. I return to the role of power in pragmatism later.

3. Pragmatists believe that binary distinctions such as art/science deconstruct. The emphasis on art and aesthetics that follows is not designed to denigrate science and technology. Rather, science and technology are necessary, at least at the end of the twentieth century, to bring about much that is artistic and aesthetically pleasing. A pragmatist who is interested in aesthetically pleasing outcomes wants her predictions, forecasts, and conceptions of consequences to be accurate and reliable because that will increase the likelihood that she will realize her conceptions of satisfaction and beauty.

4. It was the work of John McDermott that first drew my attention to the importance of aesthetics in pragmatism. Although McDermott located aesthetics at the center of Dewey's philosophy, I hesitate to use the terms *center, foremost,* or *primary* because of poststructural warnings that what is central today will be marginal tomorrow and vice versa. Aesthetics, along with power and ethics and alternative rhetorical strategies, continually circulate, I submit, as we trace out conceivable practical consequences. I start my reading of pragmatism with aesthetics because at the beginning and end of the day we are faced with questions of what constitutes satisfactory and desirable outcomes and whether they have been secured.

5. Philip Jackson (1995) makes a parallel argument specifically in the context of education. Whereas educational achievement has traditionally been conceptualized in terms of cognitive outcomes, it is arguable that art and aesthetic education can make important contributions to these outcomes. Jackson writes:

> With respect to the specific problem of how the arts might be used to sensitize students to the expressive dimensions of ordinary experience, the key would seem to lie in class discussions, exercises, and assignments that encouraged students to switch back and forth from a narrow focus on a particular art object or performance to a broader perspective that embraced the contents of their immediate surroundings and the fabric of their daily lives. (p. 34)

6. I thank my Teacher Education 807 class, summer 1996, in Valbonne, France, for their insights and contributions as we investigated the question of beauty in the classroom.

7. Craig Cunningham (1995) makes a dramatic observation about Dewey's pragmatism on the point of the self as artist:

> There is no "Self" to be "realized." There is nothing "*in*" the future possibilities of the self, no *intrinsic* essence, no "brute core of existence," no defining characteristic toward which to guide personal growth. The potential self is primarily characterized by *incompleteness*. . . . It is "a field of indeterminate (though not limitless) transactionality" (Calore, 1989, p. 19). (Cunningham, p. 190, emphasis in original).

The constitution of the self as a continuing inductive experiment, then, is an artistic project.

8. I address the issue of dealing with the conflicts that are generated by different notions of art and aesthetics in Chapter 11.

9. For a superb discussion of the contrast between pragmatist and formalist aesthetics, see Shusterman (1992, Chapter 1). For a discussion of the problem of structural binary distinctions in education, see Cherryholmes (1988, Chapters 3 and 7).

10. This is not dissimilar from Robert Scholes's (1989) idea of a nihilistic hermeneutics, where one attempts to acquire a deep understanding of the center of a centerless text.

CHAPTER 5

1. This is not the place to discuss in detail these research technologies or the philosophical positions upon which they rest. That has been done repeatedly and excellently elsewhere. My preferred introductions and comparisons among social science research methodologies are Fay (1983) and R. Bernstein (1977). For a discussion of these approaches to research in terms of construct validity, see Cherryholmes (1988, Chapter 6). For a discussion of empiricism and critical research in the context of a specific piece of research, see Chapters 8, 9, and 10.

2. Such constructions have been extensively theorized in constitutive theories of language (see Searle, 1980, for an introduction) or the politics of representation (see M. Shapiro, 1988, for an introduction).

3. The literature on the social effects of power, ideology, gender, race, and social class on social behavior is enormous and will not be reviewed here. For some of my thoughts on power, see Cherryholmes (1988, particularly footnote 1 on page 191).

4. Leach (1995) makes an observation about Foucault and feminist thought that also holds for pragmatism. "At its worst," she writes, "[the emphasis on the normative] reinscribes the complicity between extant discourses and the 'given' authority of the normative. Part of the appeal of Foucault for feminism is his commitment to unmasking this complicity" (p. 131). It is likewise important for

pragmatists to unmask the operation of power in the constitution of imagined consequences and their desirability.

CHAPTER 6

1. Raymond Boisvert (1995) provides an insightful reading of Dewey on democracy by pointing out that (1) "A democratic society is one which encourages 'individuality' as opposed to 'individualism'" (p. 165), where individuality "is to be measured by the distinctive manner in which a person can contribute to shared undertakings" and individualism is "assertion of self apart from others"—and therefore cannot be a democratic ideal (p. 165). (2) Democratic societies are committed to freedom and equality, where freedom is the capacity to carry out projects in practice and equality is the fact that we each are irreplaceable, that is, we are equal in our differences one from another. (3) Democracies are characterized by social mobility and fluid social relations (p. 166).

2. The holism of pragmatism, to be discussed shortly, continually presses for the deconstruction of binary distinctions such as text/context.

3. When pragmatists acknowledge that they are fallibilists, they place themselves at a rhetorical disadvantage compared to, say, empiricists who believe that controlled and systematic inquiry will get them closer to reality and foundationalists of one sort or another. (See Haack, 1993, for an account of various forms of foundationalism. What Haack calls "foundherentism" resembles the position that I describe in this section.) Pragmatists seemingly place themselves at a disadvantage compared to those who claim to have more certain argumentative foundations. The disadvantage is that pragmatists claim to "know" little in the sense of essential or foundational or universal knowledge. Of course, pragmatists believe that not only they but also their critics are fallible.

Shusterman (1992) makes a similar argument in discussing the problem of legitimating popular art: "The first [problem] is that legitimating popular art against the intellectualist critique involves waging the campaign mostly on the enemy's territory with similar weapons. For the very attempt to meet that critique involves accepting to some extent the power of its claim to require an answer" (p. 205).

4. For research methodologists, one reason that external validity is problematic is because interaction effects are unknown; the deconstruction of the text/context distinction is due to such unpredictable interactions.

5. John Holder (1995), for example, deconstructed the distinction between rational and creative thinking that has been promoted in cognitivist orientations to research and policy. He argued for a naturalistic theory of experience, following in the footsteps of Dewey's naturalized epistemology, where inquiry is always already contextualized.

6. The debates about essentialism, representationalism, and foundationalism are a bit more technical than most of the other ideas covered in this chapter. For a forceful argument on the pragmatist side, see Richard Rorty, *Philosophy and the Mirror of Nature* (1979) For criticisms of the pragmatist position see Susan Haack, *Evidence and Inquiry* (1993) and Alan Malachowski, *Reading Rorty* (1990).

7. Susan Bickford describes an antifoundational position as "theories that reject an ahistorical, absolute foundation for knowledge and, relatedly, for the human self. Antifoundationalism does not refer to a source outside of history and society to justify its knowledge claims. But since they do *make* such claims, antifoundational theories are not ungrounded; however, the grounds invoked tend to be contextual rather than transcendent" (1993, p. 105).

Jane Duran characterizes a nonfoundational and pragmatist epistemics as one that would "rely on the notion that gynocentric theory posists knowledge as coming from communities or groups of believers. . . . The emphasis is on the building up of confirmation through interpersonal relationships and the relevant discourse practices" (1993, p. 165).

8. Martin Benjamin, a philosopher and colleague, characterizes the difference between pragmatists and nonpragmatists in terms of an imaginary "gestalt" switch in their minds. If the switch is set in one position one sees the world as a pragmatist, if set in another position one sees the world as a fundamentalist or truth seeker. I believe the operative mechanism in such a "gestalt" is whether the individual has taken the linguistic turn and accepted all that it implies on the pragmatist side or reifies language on the fundamentalist side.

CHAPTER 7

1. This view parallels roughly that stated by Ian Shapiro (1990):

Science holds out the hope that we can get beyond the welter of conflicting opinions and ideological claims to the truth of a matter, that we can come to hold a set of beliefs about an entity, event, or action that is most reasonable under the circumstances. . . . Although this is difficult in practice, there is no reason to rule it out in principle. (p. 274)

The implication here is that there may be convergence to one set of beliefs that are beyond the welter of conflicting opinions. Maybe and maybe not. To hold out the idea of truth as the convergence of beliefs is to express nostalgia for the positivist and empiricist goal of speaking correctly about the world, where we all speak the language of nature. I do not find the idea of convergence to be a useful guideline for either conceptions or action. Otherwise, I find Shapiro's construction to be quite congenial.

Seigfried (1993) writes that "pragmatists do not talk of science as though it represents an independent truth-seeking mechanism but as the employment of experimental methodologies by communities of inquirers" (p. 10). And what beliefs they settle on for the moment as most reasonable to accept is, for me, what operate as truths, not Truth.

2. Lynn Nelson's (1993) pragmatic view of evidence is closely related to what beliefs are accepted as true. She wrote:

My account of evidence is pragmatic in the sense that on that view there are no pretheoretic notions of evidence, no standards or methods laid down prior to the business of constructing theories to explain and predict what we experience. Rather, it is within our various epistemological projects—in daily life, in philosophy, in politics—that notions and standards of evidence emerge, concomitantly with the unfolding of those projects. (p. 173)

3. James Marshall (1995) began an essay that was largely devoted to attacking Rorty's reading and comparison of Dewey and Foucault with this quote. For my purposes it is sufficient to note that whatever else Marshall objected to in Rorty's argument, he did not take exception to the idea that "when the notion of knowledge as representation goes . . . the lines between novels and the human sciences become blurred lines, drawn only pragmatically by existing current concerns, be they 'theoretical' or practical" (p. 139).

4. Arguments similar to these pragmatic themes have been recently made by Robert Scholes. He took the title of his book *Protocols of Reading* (1989) from Jacques Derrida: "He [Derrida] says we need them [protocols of reading] but he has never found any that satisfy him" (p. ix). Scholes contends that today's most interesting interpreters and critics employ a vague and elusive strategy that he calls nihilistic hermeneutics. It is similar in many ways to my combination of Peircean and Jamesian pragmatism. Scholes (1989) wrote:

Hermeneutics refers to the search for truth or grounded meaning in texts (or the method or principles governing that search) and *nihilistic* refers to the view that truth (or grounded meaning) can never be attained . . . nihilistic hermeneutics is indeed the paradoxical name of an impossible practice. My own view is that we need some such name—paradoxical or not—while we grope toward some new protocols of reading. (p. 57)

5. Such a viewpoint is similar to the radically relativist and self-refuting position that one belief is as good as any other, which would mean that two contradictory beliefs would be equally good.

6. On this I follow Quine's (1953/1971) concluding comment in "Two Dogmas of Empiricism":

Carnap, Lewis, and others take a pragmatic stand on the questions of choosing between language forms, scientific frameworks; but their pragmatism leaves off at the imagined boundary between the analytic and the synthetic. In repudiating such a boundary I espouse a more thorough pragmatism. Each man is given a scientific heritage plus a continuing barrage of sensory stimulation; and the considerations which guide him in warping his scientific heritage to fit his continuing sensory promptings are, where rational, pragmatic. (p. 46)

7. This argument is vulnerable, perhaps, to some of the interpretations and criticisms it advances. Some might charge, for example, that it is phallologocentric from a feminist perspective, wittingly or unwittingly oppressive from a critical viewpoint, or full of contradictions and ambiguities from the vantage of deconstruction. I am not willing to concede the substance of such charges, I do concede that this argument does not escape the kinds of interpretative and critical issues it explores with respect to other texts.

8. I thank Richard Prawat for bringing this article to my attention.

CHAPTER 8

1. Linda Alcoff's (1988) discussion of issues that separate cultural feminism from poststructural feminism, for example, provides arguments about how feminist thought can produce distinctly different readings of the same text.

CHAPTER 11

1. The text for Palincsar and Brown was their set of hypotheses and quasi-experimental intervention. The text for the three readings, was that of Palincsar and Brown. In each case text can be thought of as a concept in Peirce's formulation "as the affirmation or denial of . . . [a] concept."

CHAPTER 12

1. This is a continuation of the argument in Cherryholmes (1988).

2. My take on the meaning of what is postmodern is to read the word *modern* under erasure, to use Derrida's (1976) term. Reading a word under erasure is simultaneously to affirm and reject it; thus reading *modern* under erasure is simultaneously to affirm and reject what is modern. The law of the excluded middle that is often taught in introductory philosophy courses is not operative here. Pragmatism's concern with tracing conceivable consequences utilizes both modern *and* postmodern constructions. As a result, both modern and postmodern thought and practice are pragmatically useful.

CHAPTER 13

1. Lynn Nelson (1993) described a pragmatic account of scientific evidence that she drew from Quine's arguments:

My account of evidence is pragmatic in the sense that on that view there are no pretheoretic notions of evidence, no standards of methods laid down prior to the business of constructing theories to explain and predict what we experience. Rather, it is within our various epistemological projects—in daily life, in science, in philosophy, in politics—that notions and standards of evidence emerge, concomitantly with the unfolding of those projects. (p. 173)

This view of evidence is in line with the inductive, fallibilistic, contextual, and external validity characteristics, among others, of pragmatism, that were outlined in Chapter 5.

CHAPTER 14

1. This parallels the discussion in Chapters 7 and 11 on the point that what counts as true is the result of someone (Berger and Luckman's "says who?") tracing the conceivable practical consequences of some idea or practice (determining what is "really" going on).

2. Educational success operates as a transcendental signified whose meaning is continually deferred in the discourses on educational change and reform.

3. There is a broad parallel between innovations and institutional developments and speech acts and language that Mary Leach (1995) captures in her exploration of feminist and Deweyan arguments. She writes: "There is no way to free ourselves wholesale from custom and tradition [institutional context], the mind is not open to entertain *any* thought or belief whatever [innovation]. Indeed, it is understood that the very language with which one does the 'casting off' will be a collection of inherited languages" (p. 126).

4. This line of argument parallels what James Campbell (1992) calls pragmatic social thought, which strongly asserts the social and communal aspects of pragmatism.

What this [Deweyan pragmatism] bodes for the future of democracy is clear: an ongoing process of reinterpretation and revision, of specific expansions and specific contractions in its scope, an ongoing process of conceptual reconstruction. What this bodes for the future of political discourse is also clear. We need to turn our focus away from the abstractions of definition and the limitations of tradition to an emphasis upon the unexplored possibilities inherent in our political ideas. (p. 67)

What Campbell is saying, when applied to Fullan's argument about institutional development, is that it should be reconstructive, open-ended, expansive, experimental, and, I might add, aesthetic and artistic.

EPILOGUE

1. There is a flavor of determinism in the limitations that we encounter and a bit of free will in making our choices, within the degrees of freedom that we have. A determinism/free-will distinction also is discarded in this line of thinking.

APPENDIX A

1. Cornel West, however, chose to emphasize the role of Ralph Waldo Emerson when he wrote: "Emerson's dominant theses of individuality, idealism, voluntarism, optimism, amelioration, and experimentation prefigure those of American pragmatism" (1989, 35). John Patrick Diggins (1994) began his account of pragmatism with Henry Adams.

APPENDIX B

1. Macke continues, "[Pragmatism's] primary original contribution concerns the experience of creative work (both verb and noun). . . . Pragmatism is about the genealogy of performance" (1995, p. 159).
2. In the language of research methodology, pragmatists are primarily interested in questions of external validity: Are research findings generalizable to other times and settings?

References

Alcoff, L. (1988). Cultural feminism versus poststructuralism: The identity crisis in feminist theory. *Signs: Journal of Women in Culture and Society, 13*(3), 405–427.

Alexander, T. (1987). *John Dewey's theory of art, experience and nature: The horizons of feeling.* Albany: State University of New York Press.

Alexander, T. (1995). Educating the democratic heart: Pluralism, traditions and the humanities. In J. Garrison (Ed.), *The new scholarship on Dewey* (pp. 75–92). Boston: Kluwer Academic Publishers.

Anyon, J. (1980). Social class and school knowledge. *Curriculum Inquiry, 11*(1), 3–41.

Apthorpe, R. (1985). Modernization. In A. Kuper & J. Kuper (Eds.), *The social science encyclopedia* (pp. 532–533). New York: Routledge.

Belenky, M. F., Clinchy, B. M., Goldberger, N. R., & Terule, J. (1986). *Women's ways of knowing: The development of self, voice, and mind.* New York: Basic Books.

Berger, P., & Luckmann, T. (1966). *The social construction of reality.* Garden City, NY: Doubleday.

Berlin, I. (1990, September 27). Joseph de Maistre and the origins of fascism. *New York Review of Books*, pp. 59–63.

Bernstein, B. (1977). Social class, language, and socialisation. In J. Karabel & A. H. Halsey, (Eds.), *Power and ideology in education* (pp. 473–486). New York: Oxford University Press.

Bernstein, R. (1989). Pragmatism, pluralism and the healing of wounds. *American Philosophical Association Proceedings, 63*, 5–18.

Bickford, S. (1993). Why we listen to lunatics: Antifoundational theories and feminist politics. *Hypatia, 8*(2), 104–123.

Bloom, B., Englelhart, A., Furst, W., Hill, W., and Krathwohl, C. (1956). *Taxonomy of educational objectives.* New York: McKay.

Boisvert, R. (1995). John Dewey: An "old-fashioned" reformer. In J. Garrison (Ed.), *The new scholarship on Dewey* (pp. 157–173). Boston: Kluwer Academic Publishers.

Bordo, S. (1987). The Cartesian masculinization of thought. In S. Harding & J. F. O'Barr (Eds.), *Sex and scientific inquiry* (pp. 247–264). Chicago: University of Chicago Press.

Calore, G. (1989). Towards a naturalistic metaphysics of temporality: A synthesis of John Dewey's later thought. *The Journal of Speculative Philosophy, 3*(1), 12–25.

Campbell, J. (1992). *The community reconstructs: The meaning of pragmatic social thought.* Chicago: University of Illinois Press.

Cherryholmes, C. H. (1988). *Power and criticism: Poststructural investigations in education*. New York: Teachers College Press.

Cherryholmes, C. (1989). Power and criticism: Afterthoughts and responses. *Journal of Curriculum Theorizing, 9*(1), 205–218.

Cook, T. D., & Campbell, D. T. (1979). *Quasi-experimentation: Design and analysis for field settings*. Boston: Houghton Mifflin.

Cunningham, C. (1995). Dewey's metaphysics and the self. In J. Garrison (Ed.), *The new scholarship on Dewey* (pp. 175–192). Boston: Kluwer Academic Publishers.

Dahl, R. (1957). The concept of power. In N. Polsby, R. Dentler, & P. Smith (Eds.), *Politics and social life* (pp. 106–118). Boston: Houghton Mifflin.

Davidson, D. (1985). On the very idea of a conceptual scheme. In J. Rajchman & C. West (Eds.), *Post-analytic philosophy* (pp. 129–144). New York: Columbia University Press.

Derrida, J. (1976). *Of grammatology*. Baltimore: Johns Hopkins University Press.

Derrida, J. (1990). *Limited inc*. Evanston, IL: Northwestern University Press.

Derrida, J. (1996). Remarks on deconstruction and pragmatism. In C. Mouffe (Ed.), *Deconstruction and pragmatism* (pp. 77–88). New York: Routledge.

Dewey, J. (1980). *Art as experience*. New York: G. P. Putnam's Sons. (Original work published 1934)

Dewey, J. (1986). *Logic: The theory of inquiry*. New York: Holt. (Original work published 1938)

Dewey, J. (1989). The development of American pragmatism. In H. S. Thayer, (Ed.), *Pragmatism: The classic writings*. Indianapolis, IN: Hackett. (Original work published 1931)

Dewey, J. (1953). *Essays in experimental logic*. New York: Dover.

Diggins, J. P. (1994). *The promise of pragmatism: Modernism and the crisis of knowledge and authority*. Chicago: University of Chicago Press.

Dreyfus, H. L., & P. Rabinow. (1983). *Michel Foucault: Beyond structuralism and hermeneutics*. Chicago: University of Chicago Press.

Duran, J. (1993). The intersection of pragmatism and feminism. *Hypatia, 8*(2), 159–171.

Eagleton, T. (1983). *Literary theory: An introduction*. Minneapolis: University of Minnesota Press.

Ellsworth, E. (1989). Why doesn't this feel empowering? Working through the repressive myths of critical pedagogy. *Harvard Educational Review, 59*(3), 297–324.

Fay, B. (1983). *Social theory and political practice*. London: George Allen & Unwin.

Fesmire, S. A. (1995). Educating the moral artist: Dramatic rehearsal in moral education. In J. Garrison (Ed.), *The new scholarship on Dewey* (pp. 45–60). Boston: Kluwer Academic Publishers.

Foucault, M. (1972). *The archeology of knowledge*. New York: Pantheon.

Foucault, M. (1973). History, discourse, and discontinuity. *Salmagundi, 20*(Summer–Fall), 225–248.

Foucault, M. (1980a). *Language, counter-memory, practice*. Ithaca, NY: Cornell University Press.

Foucault, M. (1980b). *Power/knowledge: Selected interviews and other writings, 1972–1977*. New York: Pantheon.

Foucault, M. (1991). Questions of method. In G. Burchell, C. Gordon, & P. Miller (Eds.), *The Foucault effect: Studies in governmentality* (pp. 73–86). Chicago: University of Chicago Press. (Original work published 1980)

Fraser, N. (1989). *Unruly practices: Power, discourse, and gender in contemporary social theory.* Minneapolis: University of Minnesota Press.

Fullan, M. G. (1991). *The new meaning of educational change.* New York: Teachers College Press.

Garrison, J. (Ed.). (1995). *The new scholarship on Dewey.* Boston: Kluwer Academic Publishers.

Garrison, J. (1997). *Dewey and eros: Wisdom and desire in the art of teaching.* New York: Teachers College Press.

Giddens, A. (1979). *Central problems in social theory: Action, structure and contradiction in social analysis.* Berkeley: University of California Press.

Gloversmith, F. (1984). Autonomy theory: Ortega, Roger Fry, Virginia Woolf. In F. Gloversmith (Ed.), *The theory of reading* (pp. 147–158). Totawa, NJ: Barnes & Noble.

Greene, M. (1972). Curriculum and consciousness. In A. Bellack & H. Kliebard (Eds.), *Curriculum and evaluation* (pp. 237–253). Berkely, CA: McCutchan.

Gunn, G. (1992). *Thinking across the American grain: Ideology, intellect, and the new pragmatism.* Chicago: University of Chicago Press.

Haack, S. (1993). *Evidence and inquiry: Towards reconstruction in epistemology.* Cambridge, MA: Blackwell.

Habermas, J. (1976). The analytical theory of science and dialectics. In T. W. Adorno (Ed.), *The positivist dispute in German sociology* (pp. 131–162). New York: Harper & Row.

Habermas, J. (1979). *Communication and the evolution of society.* Boston: Beacon.

Hall, D. (1994). *Richard Rorty: Prophet and poet of the new pragmatism.* Albany: State University of New York Press.

Harding, S. (1987). *Feminism and methodology: Social science issues.* Bloomington: Indiana University Press.

Havel, V. (1992, March 1). The end of the modern era. *New York Times*, p. E 15.

Henderson, J. (1989). Reflections on an important but unfinished poststructural essay. *The Journal of Curriculum Theorizing, 8*(4), 135–142.

Holder, J. (1995). An epistemological foundation for thinking: A Deweyan approach. In J. Garrison (Ed.), *The new scholarship on Dewey* (pp. 7–24). Boston: Kluwer Academic Publishers.

Huberman, M. (1983). Recipes for busy kitchens. *Knowledge: Creation, Diffusion, Utilization, 4,* 10.

Jackson, P. W. (1995). If we took Dewey's aesthetics seriously, how would the arts be taught? In J. Garrison (Ed.), *The new scholarship on Dewey* (pp. 25–34). Boston: Kluwer Academic Publishers.

James, W. (1981). *Pragmatism.* Cambridge: Harvard University Press. (Original work published 1907)

Kerlinger, F. (1973). *Foundations of behavioral research.* New York: Holt, Rinehart & Winston.

Knapp, S., & Michaels, W. B. (1985). A reply to Rorty: What is pragmatism? In

W. J. T. Mitchell, *Against theory: Literary studies and the new pragmatism* (pp. 139–146). Chicago: University of Chicago Press.

Kuhn, T. (1972). *The structure of scientific revolutions.* Cambridge, MA: Harvard University Press.

Labaree, D. (1997). *How to succeed in school without really learning: The credentials race in American education.* New Haven, CT: Yale University Press.

Laclau, E. (1996). Deconstruction, pragmatism, hegemony. In C. Mouffe (Ed.), *Deconstruction and pragmatism* (pp. 47–68). New York: Routledge.

Leach, M. (1995). (Re)searching Dewey for feminist imaginaries: Linguistic continuity, discourse and gossip. In J. Garrison (Ed.), *The new scholarship on Dewey* (pp. 123–138). Boston: Kluwer Academic Publishers.

Leffers, M. R. (1993). Pragmatists Jane Addams and John Dewey inform the ethic of care. *Hypatia, 8*(2), 64–77.

Lentricchia, F. (1990). In place of an afterword—Someone reading. In F. Lentricchia & T. McLaughlin (Eds.), *Critical Terms for Literary Study* (pp. 321–338). Chicago: University of Chicago Press.

Lilla, M. (1998, June 25). The politics of Jacques Derrida. *The New York Review of Books,* pp. 36–41.

Loux, M. J. (1996). Essentialism. In R. Audi (Ed.), *The Cambridge dictionary of philosophy* (pp. 241–243). Cambridge, UK: Cambridge University Press.

Luke, C. (1992). Feminist politics in radical pedagogy. In C. Luke & J. Gore (Eds), *Feminisms and Critical Pedagogy* (pp. 25–53). New York: Routledge.

Macke, F. J. (1995). Pragmatism reconsidered: John Dewey and Michel Foucault on the consequences of inquiry. In L. Langsdorf & A. R. Smith (Eds.), *Recovering pragmatism's voice: The classical tradition, Rorty, and the philosophy of communication* (pp. 155–178). Albany: State University of New York Press.

Malachowski, A. (Ed.). (1990). *Reading Rorty.* Cambridge, MA: Blackwell.

Margolis, J. (1986). *Pragmatism without foundations: Reconciling realism and relativism.* New York: Blackwell.

Marris, P. (1975). *Loss and change.* New York: Anchor Press/Doubleday.

Marshall, J. (1995). On what we may hope: Rorty on Dewey and Foucault. In J. Garrison (Ed.), *The new scholarship on Dewey* (pp. 139–155). Boston: Kluwer Academic Publishers.

Maxcy, S. J. (1991). *Educational leadership: A critical pragmatic perspective.* New York: Bergin & Garvey.

Maxcy, S. J. (1995). *Democracy, chaos, and the new school order.* Thousand Oaks, CA: Corwin.

McDermott, J. J. (Ed.). (1981). *The philosophy of John Dewey.* Chicago: University of Chicago Press.

McGowan, J. (1991). *Postmodernism and its critics.* Ithaca, NY: Cornell University Press.

McLaughlin, T. (1990). Introduction. In F. Lentricchia & T. McLaughlin (Eds.), *Critical terms for literary study* (pp. 1–8). Chicago: University of Chicago Press.

Murphy, J. (1990). *Pragmatism: From Peirce to Davidson.* Boulder, CO: Westview.

Nelson, J., Megill, A., & McCloskey, D. (Eds.). (1987). *Rhetoric of the human sciences.* Madison: University of Wisconsin Press.

Nelson, L. (1993). A question of evidence. *Hypatia, 8*(2), 172–189.

Palincsar, A., & Brown, A. (1984). Reciprocal teaching of comprehension-fostering and comprehension-monitoring activities. *Cognition and Instruction, 1*(2), 117–175.

Pappas, G. F. (1993). Dewey and feminism: The affective relationships in Dewey's ethics. *Hypatia, 8*(2), 78–95.

Patterson, J., Purkey, S., & Parker, J. (1986). *Productive school systems for a nonrational world.* Alexendria, VA: Association for Supervision and Curriculum Development.

Peirce, C. S. (1984). Review of Nichols *A Treatise On Cosmology, The Monist,* XV (April, 1905). In H. S. Thayer, (1984), *Meaning and action: A critical history of pragmatism* (pp. 494–495) Indianapolis: IN: Hackett Publishing Company. (Original work published 1905)

Peirce, C. S. (1989). How to make our ideas clear. In H. S. Thayer (Ed.), *Pragmatism: The classic writings* (pp. 79–100). Indianapolis: Hackett Publishing Company. (Original work published 1878)

Popper, K. (1959). *The logic of scientific discovery.* London: Hutchinson.

Prado, C. G. (1987). *The limits of pragmatism.* Atlantic Highlands, NJ: Humanities Press International.

Quine, W. V. O. (1971). Two dogmas of empiricism. In *From a logical point of view* (pp. 21–43). Cambridge, MA: Harvard University Press. (Original work published 1953)

Quine, W. V. O. (1992). *Pursuit of truth* (rev. ed.). Cambridge, MA: Harvard University Press.

Rajchman, J., & West, C. (Eds.). (1985). *Post-analytic philosophy.* New York: Columbia University Press.

Rooney, P. (1993). Feminist-pragmatist revisionings of reason, knowledge, and philosophy. *Hypatia, 8*(2), 15–37.

Rorty, R. (Ed.). (1967). *The linguistic turn.* Chicago: University of Chicago Press.

Rorty, R. (1979). *Philosophy and the mirror of nature.* Princeton, NJ: Princeton University Press.

Rorty, R. (1982). *The consequences of pragmatism.* Minneapolis: University of Minnesota Press.

Rorty, R. (1985). Philosophy without principles. In W. J. T. Mitchell (Ed.), *Against theory: Literary studies and the new pragmatism* (pp. 132–138). Chicago: University of Chicago Press.

Rorty, R. (1990). Introduction. In J. P. Murphy, *Pragmatism: From Peirce to Davidson.* Boulder, CO: Westview.

Rorty, R. (1991). *Objectivity, relativism, and truth: Philosophical papers* (Vol. 1). Cambridge, UK: Cambridge University Press.

Rorty, R. (1991). *Essays on Heidegger and others: Philosophical papers* (Vol. 2). Cambridge, UK: Cambridge University Press.

Rorty, R. (1996). Response to Ernesto Laclau. In Chantal Mouffe (Ed.), *Deconstruction and pragmatism* (pp. 69–76). New York: Routledge.

Rosenthal, S. B. (1990). *Specualtive pragmatism.* LaSalle, IL: Open Court.

Rudner, R. (1966). *Philosophy of social science.* Englewood Cliffs, NJ: Prentice-Hall.

Said, E. (1975). *Beginnings: Intention and method.* New York: Basic Books.

Salmon, W. (1963). *Logic.* Englewood Cliffs, NJ: Prentice-Hall.

Sarason, S. (1990). *The predictable failure of educational reform.* San Francisco: Jossey-Bass.

Scholes, R. (1985). *Textual power.* New Haven, CT: Yale University Press.

Scholes, R. (1989). *Protocols of reading.* New Haven, CT: Yale University Press.

Searle, J. (1980). *Speech act theory and pragmatics.* Boston: Kluwer Academic Publishers.

Seigfried, C. H. (1993). Shared communities of interest: Feminism and pragmatism. *Hypatia, 8*(2), 1–14.

Selden, R. (1989). *Practicing theory and reading literature.* Lexington: University of Kentucky Press.

Shapiro, I. (1990). *Political criticism.* Berkeley, CA: University of California Press.

Shapiro, M. (1988). *The politics of representation: Writing practices in biography, photography, and policy analysis.* Madison: University of Wisconsin Press.

Shusterman, R. (1992). *Pragmatist aesthetics: Living beauty, rethinking art.* Cambridge, MA: Blackwell.

Shusterman, R. (1997). *Practicing philosophy: Pragmatism and the philosophical life.* New York: Routledge.

Silverman, H. (1994). *Textualities: Between hermeneutics and deconstruction.* New York: Routledge.

Skrtic, T. M. (1991). *Behind special education: A critical analysis of professional culture and school organization.* Denver, CO: Love Publishing.

Smith, J. E. (1992). *America's philosophical vision.* Chicago: University of Chicago Press.

Stanley, W. B. (1992). *Curriculum for utopia: Social reconstruction and critical pedagogy in the postmodern era.* Albany: State University of New York Press.

Stuhr, J. (1997). *Genealogical pragmatism: Philosophy, experience, and community.* Albany: State University of New York Press.

Thayer, H. S. (1981). *Meaning and action: A critical history of pragmatism.* Indianapolis, IN: Hackett Publishing Company.

Tyler, R. (1949). *Basic principles of curriculum and instruction.* Chicago: University of Chicago Press.

Veeser, H. A. (1988). *The new historicism.* New York: Routledge.

Vygotsky, L. S. (1978). *Mind in society: The development of higher psychological processes* (M. Cole, V. John-Steiner, S. Scribner, & E. Souberman, Eds. and Trans.). Cambridge, MA: Harvard University Press.

West, C. (1989). *The American evasion of philosophy: A genealogy of pragmatism.* Madison: University of Wisconsin Press.

Westbrook, R. (1991). *John Dewey and American democracy.* Ithaca, NY: Cornell University Press.

Wiener, P. (1973). Pragmatism. In *Dictionary of the history of ideas.* New York: Charles Scribner's Sons.

Wise, A. (1977). Why educational policies often fail: The hyperrationalization hypothesis. *Curriculum Studies, 9*(1), 43–57.

Wood, D. (1987). Beyond deconstruction? In A. P. Griffith (Ed.), *Contemporary French philosophy* (pp. 175–194). New York: Cambridge University Press.

Index

143

About the Author

Cleo H. Cherryholmes is Professor of Teacher Education and Coordinator of the Master of Arts in Curriculum and Teaching degree program at Michigan State University. He received his bachelor's degree from Yale University, master's degree from Emporia State University, and his doctorate from Northwestern University. His interest in curriculum theory, educational philosophy, politics, and contemporary social theory can be found in *Power and Criticism: Poststructural Investigations in Education* and numerous articles. He has published in the *American Educational Research Journal, Educational Researcher, Journal of Curriculum Studies, Curriculum Inquiry, American Journal of Education, Journal of Education, Theory and Research in Social Education, Social Education,* and *Theory into Practice.* He has recently taught curriculum theory, educational philosophy, philosophy of educational research, classroom inquiry for teachers, and social studies education. He continues to explore pragmatism, aesthetics, knowledge, and power in educational thought and practice.